THE COMPLETE BOOK OF
Needlework And
Embroidery

THE COMPLETE BOOK OF

Needlework And Embroidery

WINIFRED BUTLER

G. P. Putnam's Sons, New York

FIRST AMERICAN EDITION, 1967

Library of Congress Catalog
Card Number: 67-29481

PRINTED IN THE UNITED STATES OF AMERICA

Contents

Part Four: Home Makes

13 *Soft Furnishings*   117

    CURTAINS; BEDSPREADS; CUSHIONS.

14 *Upholstery*   131

    CHAIR SEAT COVERS; COVERED BEDHEAD; LOOSE COVERS.

15 *Lampshade Making*   138

    MATERIALS; PATTERNS FOR VARIOUS SHAPES.

16 *Rugmaking*   144

    VARIOUS TECHNIQUES INCLUDING KNOTTED PILE, LOOPED, RAG, NYLON, BRAIDED AND EMBROIDERED PATTERN FOR CONTEMPORARY RUG, OVAL EMBROIDERED RUG, STAIRCARPET, AND HEXAGON RUG.

Part Five: Knitting and Crochet

17 *Knitting*   155

    DIAGRAMS AND PATTERNS FOR CLASSIC GARMENTS FOR ALL THE FAMILY.

18 *Crochet*   170

TECHNIQUE: ILLUSTRATIONS AND PATTERNS FOR MOTIF AND BORDER.

Part Six: Jiffy Gifts

19 *Jiffy Gifts*   181

    TO KNIT OR SEW, INCLUDING BAZAAR MAKES AND TOYS.

Index   193

Illustrations

Introduction

NEEDLEWORK has always been a popular hobby, but nowadays there is not much leisure time, so modern stitchery has to be quick and easy to complete. It must be practical too, resulting in the saving of money. This book is written with both these facts in mind.

In addition to embroidery, you will find a variety of needle-crafts, including dressmaking, rugmaking, knitting and crochet, with new ideas of implementing traditional techniques.

To ensure success and satisfaction one should use the correct stitches and methods. It is best to begin with a simple piece of work to practise the stitches and familiarize yourself with the basic principles of sewing. Each technique is clearly explained and working diagrams are given for every stitch. With this knowledge you will have the satisfaction of making exactly what you need for yourself or for your home.

Each chapter contains information on the most suitable materials for the different kinds of needlework and practical examples are given throughout. If instructions are followed in detail you will be able to complete any item you choose without difficulty.

The essential tools for needlework are not expensive. You will need sharp scissors, a steel-lined thimble, a strong tape measure and straight needles – this applies to sewing or knitting and crochet.

Besides being a pleasant relaxation, needlework is a rewarding occupation and affords everyone the opportunity of being creative. I hope this book will inspire you to enlarge on the original ideas and enable you to enjoy many happy hours of sewing.

Part 1

BASIC SEWING AND EMBROIDERY

CHAPTER I

Simple Sewing

I F you are a complete beginner you will be able to make any one of the items in this section. They are all made from straight strips, using only easy-to-sew basic stitches.

BATHMAT

Diagram 1. Only two short seams are involved in the making of this very practical bathmat. It is lined with foam rubber sheeting which is easily removed through the back opening.

Diagram 1

Materials: 1 yard of 40-inch-wide towelling; plastic foam sheeting, 20 by 34 inches; matching sewing-thread and sewing-needle.

Measurement: 20 by 34 inches.

To Make: Fold selvedge edges of towelling to centre as shown in diagram 2, with the right sides inside.

Diagram 2. Pin raw edges together. Join each short end

with back-stitch, 1 inch from edge (see diagram 3). Remove pins and turn out to right side. Insert foam pad.

Diagram 3 : Back-Stitch. This consists of a continuous line of small stitches on the right side and long overlapping stitches on the wrong side. It makes a strong seam and is the nearest equivalent to machine-stitching. Work from right to left. Insert needle ⅛ inch to the right of thread and bring it out ⅛ inch to the left of thread. For next stitch take needle down at beginning of previous stitch.

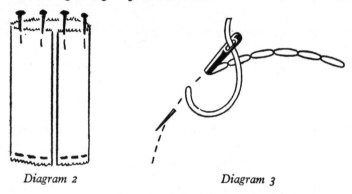

Diagram 2   *Diagram 3*

FELT TABLE COVER

Diagram 4. This is an excellent way of protecting the surface of tables when children are playing games. Felt is available in gay colours and comes in various widths, up to 72 inches.

Diagram 4

Materials : Felt large enough to overlap table 3 inches all around. Cotton fringe 2 inches wide, for edge. Matching sewing-thread.

To Make : Round off the corners of felt by placing a circular object 1 inch from tip along side edges. Place the felt on a flat surface and pin the fringe all around, ½ inch from the edge, and easing fringe round corners. Machine-stitch or back-stitch (see diagram 3) the fringe to the felt, joining ends of fringe neatly.

TRAYCLOTH

Diagram 5. A piece of material from your bits box can be made into a useful traycloth with the simple addition of scalloped bias binding.

Diagram 5

Materials: Fabric 15 by 22 inches; 2¼ yards of ready-scalloped bias binding; matching sewing-thread.

To Make: Round off the corners of fabric by placing a coin ½ inch from tip along side edges. Bind edges with scalloped bias (see bias binding below). Press work well.

Bias Binding: Open out the folded edge of bias and pin bias to fabric, right sides inside and raw edges together. Sew bias to fabric along the fold line with running stitch (see diagram 6) or machine-stitch. Join ends of binding on wrong side. Fold bias over to the wrong side and hem the folded edge over the seam line. See diagram 8 for hemming.

Diagram 6: Running-Stitch. This stitch is used for light seams and for gathering. Work from right to left. Weave needle in and out of fabric, feeding the fabric on to the needle-point with the left hand. Make the stitches even

Diagram 6

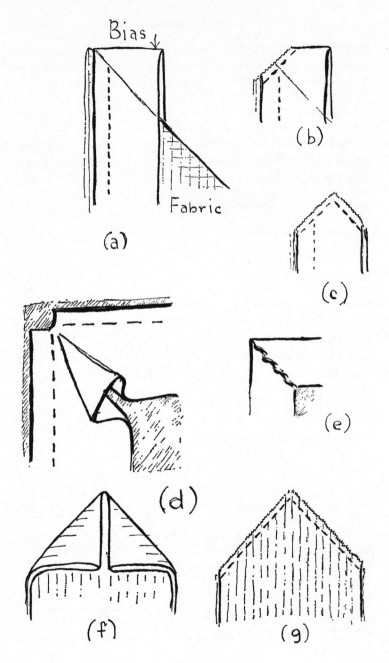

Bias

Fabric

(a)

(b)

(c)

(d)

(e)

(f)

(g)

Diagram 7

on both sides of the fabric and do not remove needle from fabric until the entire length is worked – ease the fabric off the other end of the needle as the work proceeds. Length of stitch may vary from $\frac{1}{8}$ inch on fine fabric to $\frac{1}{4}$ inch on coarse fabric.

Diagram 7 : Mitring. This enables the fabric to lie flat at corners.

Bias Binding : Take binding to corner of fabric up to seam margin. Fold fabric diagonally and bias at right angles (*a*) then fold corner in diagonally up to seam and crease with thumb-nail. Sew along crease then cut away surplus (*b*). Fold and sew opposite corner of bias in the same way (*c*). *Facing :* Take facing to corner of fabric up to seam margin. Clip corner and continue sewing other side, leaving fullness in centre (*d*). Turn facing inside, fold in excess diagonally to corner and hem fold (*e*). *Blanket Binding :* Open out binding and fold across width on wrong side (the fold line should be the extremity of corner). Fold doubled fabric diagonally to centre and crease fold with thumb-nail. (*f*) Sew along fold then trim away excess. Fold opposite side in the same way (*g*) and complete to match.

Diagram 8 : Hemming. Pick up one thread from fabric immediately below fold and take needle up through edge of fold at an angle. Do not draw stitches up tightly and make stitches $\frac{1}{4}$ inch apart.

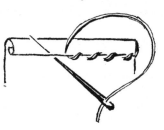

Diagram 8

BABY BLANKET

Diagram 9. This cosy blanket can be quickly made from a woollen remnant, bound with ready-folded satin binding.

Materials : A piece of woollen cloth, 25 by 32 inches;

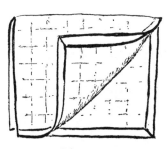

Diagram 9

3¼ yards of matching blanket binding; matching sewing-thread.

To Make: Pin fold of binding to fabric edge all round to check position of each corner, allowing ½-inch seam extensions on first corner. Mark position of corners then remove binding. Mitre each corner as shown in diagram 7 (*f*) and (*g*).

Replace ribbon binding over fabric, ensuring that the edge of fabric is up to the fold inside binding. Sew binding to fabric with stab-stitch through all three layers, near edge of binding (see diagram 10).

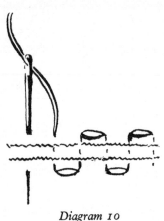

Diagram 10

Diagram 10: Stab-Stitch. This is used for sewing more than two layers together or when fabric is too thick for the needle to pass in and out in the one movement. Take needle at right angles through all layers from front to back of work, then return needle at right angles from back to front of work. Keep the stitches even throughout, varying from ⅛ inch to ¼ inch apart.

MOHAIR BERET

Diagram 11. If you have been given an extra mohair scarf you can make this snug beret in a jiffy. The scarf used for the original beret measured 10 by 46 inches and was bought in a chain store, quite inexpensively.

Materials: A mohair scarf or mohair fabric 10 by 46 inches; 24 inches of 1-inch-wide elastic; matching sewing-thread.

Measurement: To fit average-size head.

To Make: Fold the scarf in half (fringed ends together) and join the short ends together 7 inches from fringe with back-stitch (see diagram 3). If you are using a plaid scarf make sure that the pattern matches at the seam.

Diagram 11

Cut off fringed ends, 1 inch below fringing. Then cut away surplus material up to ½ inch from the seam.

Tassel: Work running-stitch (see diagram 6) ½ inch below the fringe on each strip and gather up tightly into a circle. Fasten off securely.

Gather one long edge of main section in the same way and insert the gathered end of tassel in this section before drawing up the thread. Sew tassel from side to side to secure it in position.

Overlap the ends of elastic, making a circle to fit head, then oversew the double elastic each side. See diagram 12.

Diagram 12: Oversewing. Work from right to left. Take needle over the edge and insert it diagonally through both edges. Keep the stitches close together.

Diagram 12

Place elastic circle inside lower edge of beret and turn lower edge over the elastic. Hem the inside edge as shown in diagram 8.

PLACE MAT

Diagram 13. These dainty mats are easily made and will enhance any table setting. They are made from crisp organza, trimmed with ribbon-threaded lace.

Diagram 13

Materials: For each mat – a piece of organza, 18 by 25 inches; 13 inches of 1½-inch-wide lace trimming with centre beading (for ribbon); ½ yard of ¼-inch-wide nylon ribbon; matching nylon thread.

Measurements: 12¼ by 17½ inches.

To Make: Fold organza in half across width. Join sides and lower edge together with running stitch (see diagram 6) ¼ inch from the edge, leaving a small opening at one side. Turn out to right side through opening then oversew the opening (see diagram 12).

Thread ribbon through the beading and cut off surplus. Turn in ends of ribbon-threaded lace and pin this 2 inches from one side edge. Attach lace to organza with running stitch each side of ribbon. Oversew the ends in position.

Make a small bow of remaining ribbon and sew to top edge of lace trimming. Press seams lightly with a cool iron.

SHOWER CLOTH

This is made from narrowly-hemmed nylon net, weighted all round with plastic beads. It makes a featherlight cover for a pre-laid tea-table or picnic spread, and also would be ideal to cover a pram when baby is sleeping out of doors.

Materials : A 45-inch square of nylon net; 176 plastic beads (strings of $\frac{1}{4}$-inch beads are cheap to buy in chain stores); matching nylon thread.

To Make : Turn in $\frac{1}{2}$ inch all round then turn under $\frac{1}{4}$ inch and hem. See diagram 8 for hemming. Sew beads 1 inch apart all round hem edge, beginning in the corner of cloth.

Much smaller versions of this cloth could be made from scraps of net and odd beads to cover a milk jug or sugar basin.

CHAPTER 2

Embroidery Stitches

Back-Stitch. This is worked as described in diagram 3. It is used for outlining designs or defining leaf markings and other fine lines. This stitch is used as a foundation for the following variations:

Diagram 14: Double Back-Stitch. This is used to fill the space between two lines for stems and borders. It resembles close herringbone stitch. Work from left to right. Bring the needle out on the top line, take up ⅛ inch on the lower line, from right to left, then take up ⅛ inch on the upper line, to the right of the thread. Continue in this way throughout, forming a close herringbone on the surface (*a*) and two continuous lines of back-stitch on the other side (*b*).

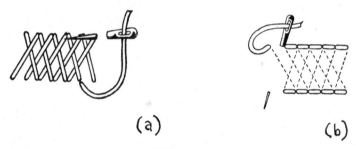

(a)   (b)

Diagram 14

This stitch is used effectively for Shadow Work. Designs are worked on transparent materials (on the wrong side) and the stitching shown through the material, with the back-stitch forming a good outline.

Diagram 15. Trace-off motif for shadow work. Ideal for dressing-table mats in delicate organdie, edged with fine lace.

Diagram 15

Diagram 16: Threaded Back-Stitch. This makes a pretty border and can be worked with a single or double threading. First work back-stitch as described in diagram 3. Pass the threaded needle up and down under the stitches alternately without piercing the material. To do this easily pass the needle-eye under the stitches instead of the point.

Diagram 17: Braid-Stitch. A decorative stitch for bold out-

Diagram 16

lines. It is best worked with a thick thread, such as perlé. Work from right to left. Bring needle out to lower edge, hold thread to the left then draw working thread under this held strand with the needle-point – thus forming a loop under the held strand. Insert needle through loop and out again over thread at lower edge. Continue in this way throughout. This stitch may be substituted for the applied braid in the design on page 36.

Diagram 17

Diagram 18: Broderie Anglaise. Consisting mainly of oval and round eyelets, this work is very suitable for baby clothes and lingerie. It should be worked in closely woven fabric and is generally embroidered in white on white material. Use a rounded thread, such as *coton-à-broder* and fine sharp scissors. First run-stitch the outline of the round or oval eyelet, then cut across the enclosed area both ways. Turn the cut sections to the wrong side with the needle and overcast over the run-stitching (*a*). As work proceeds cut away the surplus material from the wrong side. Work outlines in overcast stitch, over a laid thread, picking up only the smallest amount of material each time (*b*).

Trace-off motif (*c*). Work the small spots in padded satin stitch as shown in diagram 39.

Diagram 19: Bullion-Stitch. This consists of coils of thread which can be used effectively for flower petals and leaves in tiny motifs. Bring the needle out to right side, insert it about ¼ inch to the right of thread and bring it out again in the original spot. Twist the thread round the needle-point for the length of

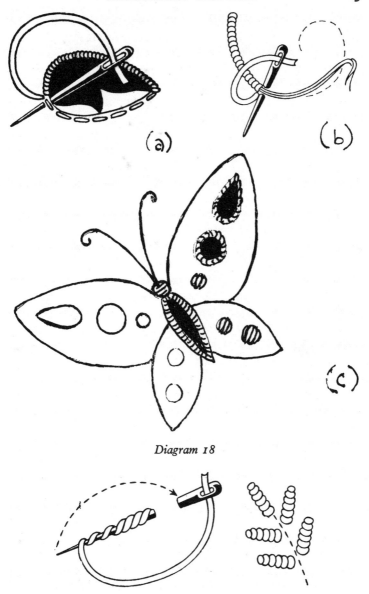

Diagram 18

Diagram 19

the stitch. Hold the coiled thread down with the left thumb and draw the needle through the coil, then insert it through the same space as indicated by the arrow.

Diagram 20: Buttonhole-Stitch. There are many versions of this stitch for embroidery, all consisting of a series of looped stitches. The open type, known as blanket-stitch, is perhaps the easiest to practise. Work this from left to right, over a doubled hem. Bring the needle out at lower edge. Hold the thread down with left thumb, insert needle at right angles above fold and bring it out at lower edge over the looped thread (*a*). Continue in this way, keeping stitches about ¼ inch apart, depending on the thickness of the material.

Grouped Buttonhole-Stitch: Work as given for blanket-stitch, but arrange the stitches in groups – slant the needle to the left for first stitch, keep it upright for centre stitch and slant it to the right for third stitch (*b*). *Cutwork* consists mainly of buttonholed outlines with some sections cut away up to the purl edge. For this type of work it is advisable to run-stitch the outline before working the buttonhole-stitch. Make sure that the purl edge of the buttonholing is along the edge where the material is to be cut away afterwards. Do not cut away any material until the embroidery has been completed. Keep the stitches very even and close together throughout (*c*). *Buttonhole Rings.* These can be worked to represent tiny flowers grouped together, such as hollyhocks (*d*).

Buttonhole Scallops. This is a useful way of finishing the edge of linens or baby clothes: Various size scallops may be drawn, using the edge of coins or kitchen utensils. To keep the scallops even throughout, use some squared paper to make a pattern as shown (*e*). Press the embroidered scallops on the wrong side before cutting away the surplus material up to the edge of stitching. Use sharp-pointed scissors and be careful not to cut the stitching.

Diagram 21: Chain-Stitch (*a*). This is a very popular embroidery stitch, with several variations. It is used for outlines and also to fill areas – both uses effectively shown in the illustration (*b*). *Cable Chain* (*c*). Begin with one chain-stitch. Hold

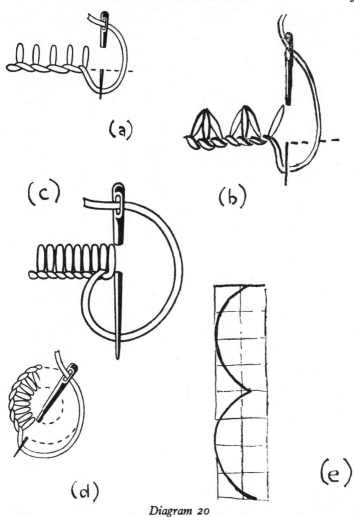

(a)

(c)

(b)

(d)

(e)

Diagram 20

the working thread with the left thumb, pass the needle under and over the held thread, then insert it at the foot of the previous loop to begin the next chain-stitch. *Magic Chain (d)*. This is worked with two contrasting threads in the needle. When making each loop pass one colour only under the needle and

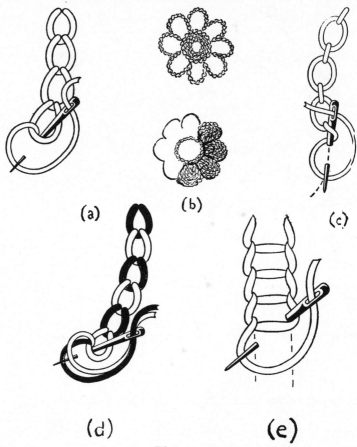

(a)

(b)

(c)

(d)   (e)

Diagram 21

pull through both threads. Work the next loop with the other colour in the same way. *Open Chain* (*e*). This stitch is begun with a chain-stitch as shown in (*a*), then the thread is held with the left thumb and the needle passed over the looped thread before the next stitch. *Twisted Chain* (*f*). Work the first loop as in (*a*). Now insert the needle at an angle outside the loop and bring it out on the working line. *Whipped Chain* (*g*). Work as given for chain stitch (*a*) first. Use a contrasting or matching

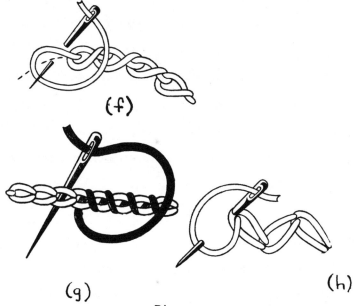

Diagram 21

thread and pass the end of needle under each chain-stitch in turn, without sewing through the material. *Zig-zag Chain* (*h*). Work first stitch from left to right for depth required. Work the next stitch from right to left, but insert the needle through the looping thread to ensure that it remains in position.

Diagram 22: Coral-Stitch. Work from right to left. Bring the thread out on the outline and hold it down with left thumb. Insert needle under the thread and through the material and bring it out over the working thread.

Diagram 23: Couching. Lay a thread along the line of the design and hold it down with the left hand. With another thread make tiny stitches at right angles over the laid thread and through

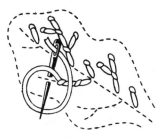

Diagram 22

the material. Do not allow the laid thread to pucker and take the ends of the laid thread to the back of the work to fasten off. This is a useful stitch for outlines and any number of threads may be couched down.

Diagram 23

Diagram 24: Cretan-Stitch.
This stitch may be worked horizontally as shown in (*a*) or opened up at an angle as shown in (*b*). It makes an effective leaf filling. Begin at centre top of shape. Take the needle to the edge of the outline on the right and bring it out over the working thread to the right of the centre. Work next stitch to the left in the same way.

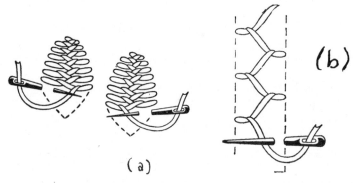

Diagram 24

Diagram 25: Cross-Stitch. For the best effect cross-stitch should be worked over counted threads on even-weave fabric, and all the top stitches should lie in the one direction. The first half of the stitch is worked from right to left as in (*a*), crossing over the same number of threads in height and width. The stitch is completed from left to right as shown in (*b*). Cross-stitch is widely used for canvas work and also for Assisi designs – this type of work is usually done on ivory linen and the cross-stitch worked in red or blue, the pattern is left plain (*c*).

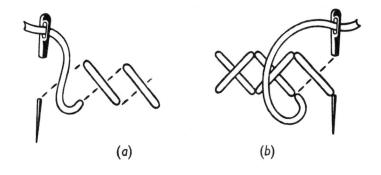

(a) (b)

(c)

Diagram 25

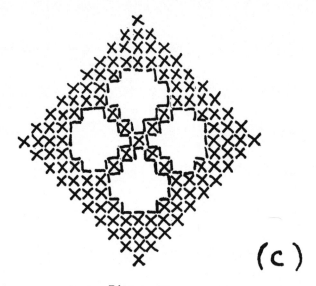

(c)

Diagram 25

Diagram 26 : Darning-Stitch. This is used to work borders or fill in areas on even-weave material. It may be worked in diagonal rows as in (*a*) or in a 'brick' pattern as in (*b*). Alternatively, the darning may be done on material with a loop weave, and attractive motifs may be worked as illustrated in (*c*).

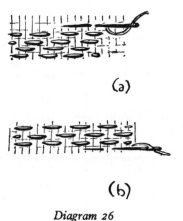

(a)

(b)

Diagram 26

Diagram 27 : Drawn-Thread Work. The basic stitch used is hem-stitch. This can only be done on even-weave material from which threads can be withdrawn. The stitching is worked over the open strands. *Hemstitch.* Allow for width of hem and draw out threads for $\frac{1}{4}$ inch. along in hem and tack fold Turn the outer edge of

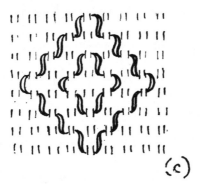

Diagram 26

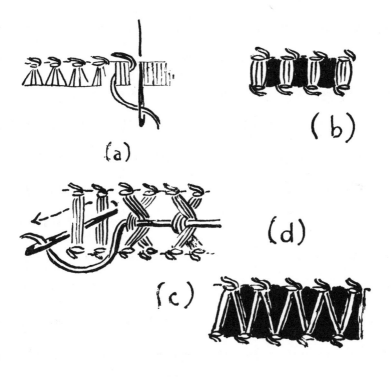

Diagram 27

drawn threads. Work from left to right. Secure thread inside hem edge. Take needle over and under four strands from right to left, draw thread through then take needle up through hem edge immediately above the opening on the right as shown in (*a*). Work the hem-stitching on the inside edge of the drawn threads and through the single fabric only (*b*). If a fringed edge is required work the hem-stitching on the inside edge only and remove remaining threads. *Laced Hem-stitch*. First work the hem-stitch as shown in (*a*) and (*b*), making the open threads about ½ inch wide. Thread needle with a strand long enough to run from end to end. Join thread to centre of drawn threads on the right. Insert needle from left to right under the second group of threads, then over and under the first group of threads and bring needle out to the left of 'crossed' groups. Continue in this way throughout (*c*). *Zig-zag Hem-stitch* (*d*). This is effected by taking up half of each group together when working the second edge of hem-stitching.

Diagram 28: Feather-Stitch. To work single feather-stitch (*a*) bring needle out at centre top. Insert needle to the right on the same level and bring it out lower down in the centre of this space and over the working thread. Work next stitch to the left and continue alternating stitches in this way throughout. For double feather-stitch (*b*) work two stitches to the right and left alternately. It is simple to work this stitch over counted threads.

Diagram 29: Fishbone-Stitch. This is a good solid

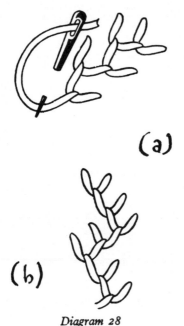

(a)

(b)

Diagram 28

stitch for filling in leaves or petals. Work sloping stitches from each side of the outline to each side of centre alternately, bring needle out below the working thread each time.

Diagram 30: Fly-Stitch. This may be worked singly (*a*) or in continuous lines (*b*). Bring needle out on the left, hold thread with left thumb, insert needle on the same level to the right and bring it out in the centre lower down, over the working thread. Insert needle again immediately below to secure the loop.

Diagram 31 : French Knot.

Diagram 29

(*a*) Bring needle out to right side, hold thread down with left thumb and twist needle twice round held thread. Still holding the thread, insert the needle back through the same place and draw the thread through the knot to the back of work. This stitch is used extensively to

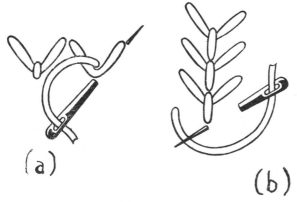

(a)

(b)

Diagram 30

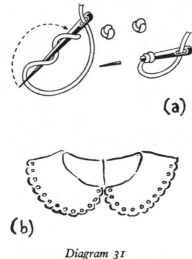

(a)

(b)

Diagram 31

enhance plain garments, for instance across the yoke of a baby gown or around the collar of a little girl's dress (*b*).

Diagram 32 : Herringbone-Stitch. There are several variations of this stitch and it makes very good borders. It is worked from left to right over double lines. First take a stitch from right to left on the top line, then take a similar stitch on the lower line (*a*). *Interlaced Herringbone.* This is worked in two separate rows with contrasting threads. First work a single row of herringbone-stitch then work a second row on top, in the spaces left in the first row (*b*). *Threaded Herringbone.* First work a single row of herringbone-stitch as shown in (*a*). With a contrast thread in needle,

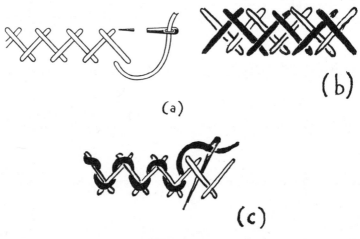

(a)

(b)

(c)

Diagram 32

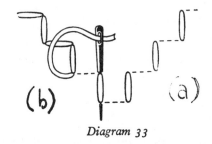

(b)

(a)

Diagram 33

and using the blunt end, weave the thread under the stitches as shown, without picking up any fabric (c).

Diagram 33: Holbein Stitch. This looks like back-stitch, but is in fact two rows of running-stitch. Work the first row from right to left (a), then fill in the spaces left on the return row from left to right (b). For best results this stitch should be worked over equal numbers of counted threads. Holbein stitch is used to outline motifs in Assisi embroidery (*see* pages 19, 20).

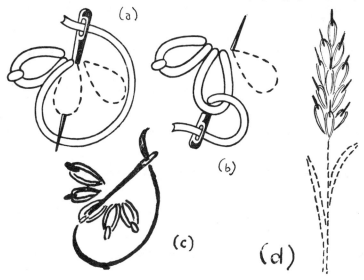

Diagram 34

Diagram 34: Lazy-Daisy Stitch. This consists of a loop, fastened at the centre lower edge with a tiny stitch as shown in (a) and (b). *Tipped-Daisy Stitch* (c). First work the lazy-daisy stitch as shown in (a) and (b), then use a contrast thread to work a longer stitch over the fastening stitch in each loop. The corn motif illustrated (*d*) could be enlarged and worked on a place mat – work the stems in back-stitch (see page 2).

Diagram 35: Long-and-Short Stitch. This is an important stitch for shaded work. The stitches alternate in length so that successive rows may be worked well into one another to avoid

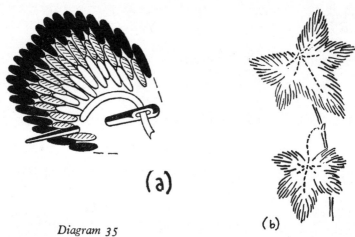

Diagram 35

hard lines (*a*). This stitch needs practice to cover large areas, but the principle can be learned in working the outline of shapes first, as shown (*b*). The stitches must follow the line of the shape throughout.

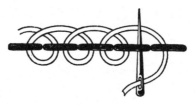

Diagram 36

Diagram 36: Pekinese Stitch. First work a row of back-stitch (see diagram 3) then interlace the stitches as shown. Use a blunt needle to avoid picking up any of the material.

Diagram 37: Raised-Rose Stitch. This makes a pretty trimming for baby's knitted garments. Begin with three or four loop stitches (*a*) secured with a back-stitch (see diagram 3). Now work around these loops in stem-stitch (see diagram 41) as shown in (*b*), graduating the height of the loops, until the rose is the required size.

Diagram 37

Diagram 38: Roumanian Stitch. Another filling stitch consisting of horizontal strands (*a*) caught down in the centre (*b*).

Diagram 39: Satin-Stitch. This must be worked very evenly and close together so that it looks like satin. Work from

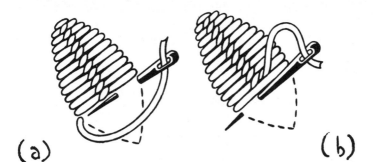

Diagram 38

side to side across the space to be covered (*a*). *Padded Satin-Stitch.* By working chain-stitch (see diagram 21) or running-stitch (see diagram 6) in the area to be covered by the satin-stitch, the work is given a raised effect, particularly suitable for *Broderie Anglaise* (see diagram 18). It is possible to slope the

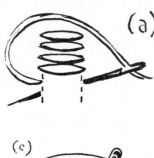

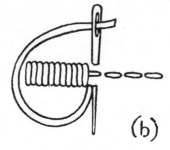

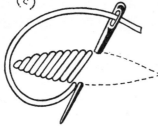

Diagram 39

satin-stitches or to work parallel rows for a different effect, as shown in (c).

Diagram 40: *Split-Stitch.* This can be used for very fine outlines or as a filling stitch for large areas. Work from left to right. Take a small stitch from right to left, inserting the point of the needle through the working thread as shown.

Diagram 41: *Stem-Stitch.* Work from left to right. Take needle through the working outline from right to left and bring it out in the centre of the stitch, above the working thread (a).

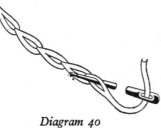

Diagram 40

This is the most popular stitch for flower-stems and markings, but it can also be used effectively to fill solid shapes as shown in the actual-size trace-off motif (b).

Diagram 42: *Straight-Stitch.* (a) A very useful stitch for working short lines, and

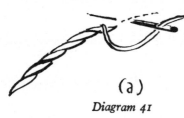

(a)

Diagram 41

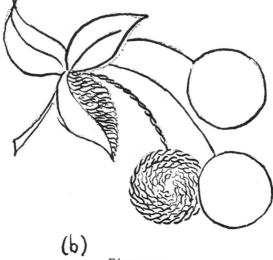

(b)

Diagram 41

more than one stitch can be worked together to obtain the required effect, as shown in motif (b).

Diagram 43: Wheatear-Stitch. Work two straight stitches in a 'v' shape and bring needle out in the centre below. Pass

Diagram 42

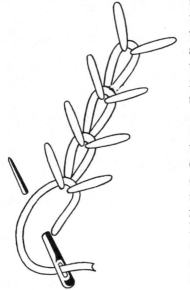

the blunt end of the needle under the straight stitches, without entering the fabric, and re-insert the needle in the centre. Bring needle out in position for the next stitch.

Diagram 44 : Woven Wheels. Suitable for filling corner sections of drawn-thread work or for decorating gingham cloths. First work straight-stitches across the area, from each corner and side. Now weave needle under and over each strand in turn as shown until the wheel is the required size.

Diagram 43

Diagram 44

EMBROIDERY HINTS

Above all, remember that practice is needed to perfect some of the stitches. Do not be discouraged if at first you do not succeed. Try out the simple stitches on a firmly woven fabric for your first attempt. Follow the instructions and diagrams very carefully and you will soon master the technique, then you will enjoy embroidery.

Understand your materials. Do not try to force thick thread

through fine fabric. Use an embroidery thread (or a number of strands of thread) to equal the thickness of the weave in the background fabric. In this way the background will be adequately covered by the working thread. Do not allow the embroidery thread to become 'fluffy' before changing to a new one. It is not advisable to use a long strand of thread, about 24 inches is sufficient.

Use crewel needles which have large eyes and allow the embroidery thread to pass easily through the fabric. The eye of the needle should be slightly larger than the thickness of the thread being used. As a rule, size 7 needle is suitable for two or three strands and size 6 for four or more strands.

If a thimble is being used, it should be steel-lined and have no rough edges to fray the working thread.

Embroidery scissors should be used; these are small (about 4 inches) and have sharp points. Keep the points inside a cork when not in use as they are easily bent and damaged.

Use an embroidery frame if a large piece of needlework is being worked. Several types are available in needlework shops. A round frame, consisting of two wooden hoops, is easy to handle and keeps the fabric taut, thus preventing puckering of stitches.

Do not make knots on the wrong side of embroidery. Each thread should be started with a few running stitches along the outline to be covered. Alternatively, the thread can be run in and out of the wrong side of previous stitches, and this is the way to finish off a thread on the wrong side of work.

Try to make up original designs for embroidery by enlarging on the patterns included with the stitches. Alternatively, interesting designs can be built up from motifs on greetings cards or illustrated seed catalogues. It is more exciting to be working original designs, choosing colours individually – in this way you can create family treasures and get greater satisfaction from sewing.

If required, transfers are available, and in different colours for dark or light fabrics. If you wish to trace a particular design for embroidery you should use embroidery carbon as this does not smudge easily.

When the embroidery is complete the work should be carefully pressed on the wrong side. Place the embroidered section over a blanket so that the stitches will not be flattened in pressing.

When embroidered articles are washed do not rub the embroidery. Squeeze the suds through gently and rinse thoroughly to remove all traces of soap. Roll the article in a dry towel before hanging and iron it when still damp.

Part 2

TECHNIQUES

CHAPTER 3

Appliqué

THIS is a bold type of embroidery, quick and easy to do because it entails only the minimum amount of stitchery. Motifs are cut out of, or made from, contrast material and applied to the background.

There are several methods of *appliqué*, depending upon the type of material being used. It is best to choose materials that do not fray too easily. For a first attempt choose felt, because this does not fray at all and need only be slip-stitched in position.

Diagram 45: Penguin Motif. Trace off this actual-size motif and use the tracing to cut out the pieces in black and white felt, making the white section ⅛ inch larger all round to fit underneath the black. Place the pieces together on a flat surface and hem the black section over the white. See diagram 8 for hemming. Now place the motif on background material and pin in position. Neatly hem all round. Finally embroider the eye and beak and feet in stem-stitch (see diagram 41) with orange thread. A group of these motifs, some reversed, would make an amusing picture for a

Diagram 45

nursery. A single motif would amuse a child if worked on a
dressing-gown.

Diagram 46: Gingham Diamonds. This is an easy material
to handle and the squared pattern makes cutting out and sewing very simple. Allow ¼-inch turnings when cutting out the
squares to required size. Turn in all round and pin to background material as shown. Hem in position (see diagram 8)
then embroider lazy-daisy flowers in the centre of every alternate diamond. See diagram 34 for embroidery. From this
simple beginning many interesting patterns may be built up –
for instance, the size of applied bits may be varied or cut from
contrasting coloured gingham.

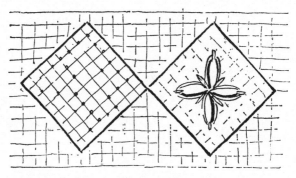

Diagram 46

If the material being used is liable to fray, then you must
work buttonhole-stitch all around the edge. Cut the motif to
the exact size for this method and work the buttonholing
evenly, keeping the stitches close together. See diagram 20 for
buttonhole-stitch. Use a thread to match the motif for this
type of work.

Diagram 47: Flower Vase. This needs delicate fabrics for
the right effect and would be most suitable for a picture. Use
silk for the flower petals, velvet for the leaf, organza for the
vase and embroidery thread for the stems. The centre of the
flower can be worked with gold threads. It is possible to en-

large the design shown here, by tracing off on to squared paper
and drawing the design on larger squares.

However, you may prefer to select a flower shape from a
catalogue and make your own simple shape for the vase.

Before cutting the delicate fabrics they should be backed
with muslin or tissue paper. To do this use a transparent adhesive and leave until quite dry before cutting out the shapes.

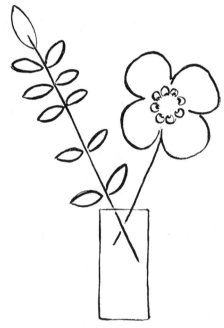

Diagram 47

First pin the flower and leaf in position on background
fabric, which should be quite plain, and hem lightly all round.
With matching thread couch down a strand thick enough to
cover the edge of the flower shape. See diagram 23 for couching. Next apply the leaf and embroider the stalks with stem-
stitch (see diagram 41). Sew beads to flower centre.

Finally place the vase section in position over the stalks and
apply to background in the same way as flower.

Diagram 48: Braid Appli-qué. This is an effective way of decorating table linens. Select a simple leaf shape from the garden, such as an ivy or oak leaf. Trace the outline on to your fabric then sew narrow braid over the outline. Narrow braid is available in a plain type (called Russian braid) which can be back-stitched through the centre (see diagram 3 for back-stitch) or a fancy type which could be lightly hemmed each side.

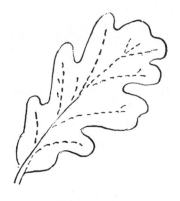

Diagram 48

Diagram 49: Flower Appliqué. Decorate a plain shopping basket with ric-rac flowers (*a*) to make an acceptable gift. Ric-rac is available in several colours and widths, so the design may be varied as required. For each flower use six scallops of

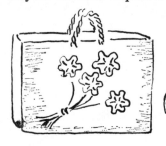

braid and join ends neatly, to form a circle. (*b*) Gather the in-side scallops together and fasten off. Stalks may be made of fine cord, knotted together at the end, or worked in couching stitch (see diagram 23), depending on the size required.

Appliqué on net – for bridal veils and christening robes. Transfer the design on to the silk or satin to be used for the motif. Lay the net over the design and work a row of running-stitch all round design. See diagram 6 for running stitch. Work chain-stitch over the running-stitch (see diagram 21) and press work. Carefully cut away the surplus material outside the motif, from wrong side of work and then cut away the net inside motif from the right side of work. If preferred, the out-line may be buttonholed (see diagram 20).

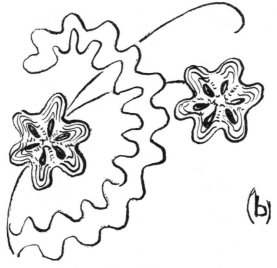

Diagram 49

CHAPTER 4

Crewel Embroidery

THIS embroidery, also called 'Jacobean' should be worked on natural twilled linen with muted shades of crewel wool.

Traditionally the designs include a tree, rising from a mound, with exotic flowers and leaves. Birds and animals are also to be found in the designs. A specimen motif is given on page 40 for you to trace off and embroider, but there are many transfers available for this type of needlework if required.

Crewel wool is a fine 2-ply wool and more than one thickness may be used if necessary. Designs can be carried out entirely in several shades of one colour. In old pieces green and brown predominated but later terracotta and blue were introduced. Use crewel needles as these have a large eye and the wool will not become fluffed in working.

Designs are generally outlined in stem- or chain-stitch, and filled with decorative stitches. In addition to the filling stitches suggested for the specimen motif other diagrams are also given for future reference.

Diagram 50. Actual-size motif to trace-off and use singly for mats, or repeated in several ways to build up borders or panels for cushions (*a*) stool (*b*) or curtains (*c*).

Embroidery: A. Centre, lazy-daisy loops (diagram 34) with straight-stitch centres (diagram 42); right edge, buttonhole-stitch (diagram 20) with french knot filling (diagram 31); left edge and tip of leaf, chain-stitch (diagram 21) with long-and-short stitch inside edge (diagram 35).

B. Stem in coral-stitch (diagram 22) and dots in satin-stitch (diagram 39).

C. Centre petal, encroaching satin-stitch (diagram 60); side

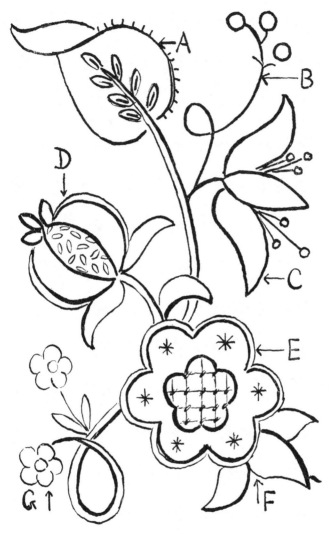

Diagram 50

(a)

(b)

(c)

Diagram 50

petals, outlined stem-stitch (diagram 41) with *tête-de-boef* filling (diagram 54); stamens in stem-stitch (diagram 41) and french knots (diagram 31).

D. Centre, seed-stitch (diagram 55); each side, herring-bone-stitch (diagram 32); tip and sides, padding satin-stitch (diagram 39b); leaves, sloping satin-stitch (diagram 39c).

E. Centre, square trellis (diagram 57) with couched outline (diagram 23); petals, outlined with two rows of stem-stitch (diagram 41) and filled with star-stitch (diagram 59).

F. Centre leaf, outlined stem-stitch (diagram 41) with continuous fly-stitch filling (diagram 30b); side leaves, cretan-stitch (diagram 24).

G. One flower and leaves, filled satin-stitch (diagram 39); other flower, edged only with satin-stitch.

Finally, work main stem in rows of stem-stitch (diagram 41) graded from a dark to a light shade.

Diagram 51: Open Buttonhole. For the first row work stitches as shown in diagram 20 (a). Alternate the successive rows by taking them over the loops of previous row.

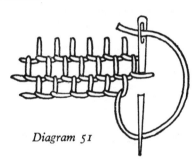

Diagram 51

Diagram 52: Basket Filling. First work the horizontal stitches. Work three rows of running-stitch, immediately under one another, leaving a space between each stitch. Arrange the

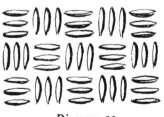

Diagram 52

next three rows to lie below the spaces left in the previous row. Continue alternating the stitches in this way until the space is filled. Now turn work round and complete the rows of running-stitch in the alternate spaces.

Diagram 53: Bokhara Couching. Bring thread out at left edge. Lay thread across work, take needle through right edge and up over laid thread.

Work small stitches over the laid thread about every $\frac{1}{2}$ inch and bring needle out at left edge again. In successive

Diagram 53

rows link the small stitches together by bringing needle up through the small stitch of previous row as shown in diagram.

Diagram 54: Tête-de-Boef Stitch. This consists of a crossed-loop stitch. Bring needle out to right side. Hold thread with left thumb, then take needle down to the left on the same level and bring it out over the working thread in the centre below. Work a small stitch over the loop.

Diagram 54

Diagram 55: Seed-Stitch. Work tiny back-stitches in all directions, working over the same stitch two or three times. See diagram 3 for back-stitch.

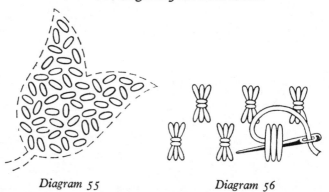

Diagram 55

Diagram 56

Diagram 56: Sheaf-Stitch. Work three vertical straight-stitches first. Bring needle out through centre and under stitches to the left. Take needle over stitches and insert it again through the centre, thus binding the stitches together as shown.

Diagram 57: Square-Trellis Stitch. Lay straight-stitches down and across the area, forming small squares. Work a small stitch over each intersection to hold the threads in position.

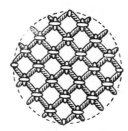

Diagram 57   *Diagram 58*

Diagram 58: Diagonal-Trellis Stitch. Work diagonal stitches across the space in each direction, forming small diamonds. Work a small cross over each intersection to hold the threads in position.

Diagram 59: Star-Stitch. Work an upright cross, then a diagonal cross and hold the threads together in the centre with a small cross-stitch. See diagram 25 for cross-stitch.

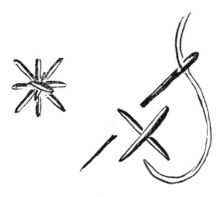

Diagram 59

Diagram 60: Encroaching Satin-Stitch. Work straight rows of satin-stitch (see diagram 39), taking the needle just between the edge of stitches in previous row each time.

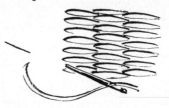

Diagram 60

CHAPTER 5

Patchwork

EVERY scrap of material can be used for this fascinating work. One can use treasured pieces to create family heirlooms. If you haven't enough pieces in your home, collect some from your friends, or buy remnants in sales.

It is best to use materials of the same type and weight for the one piece of work. For instance, all cotton or all silk. Washable and unwashable fabrics should not be mixed.

Before attempting patterns that require time and patience, you should try out a simple design with plain and patterned fabric.

Diagram 61: Patchwork Cot Cover. Size 20 by 30 inches.

You will need twenty-four 6-inch squares altogether – 12 plain and 12 patterned for a pleasing effect; a piece of lining material 21 by 31 inches; matching sewing-thread.

First join a plain and a patterned square together along one side only. Make the seam $\frac{1}{2}$ inch from the edge on the wrong side of fabric and use back-stitch (diagram 3) if sewing by hand. Join on four more squares in this way, alternating the plain and patterned fabric. Make up three more strips in the same way. Now join these strips together, reversing two of the strips to alternate

Diagram 61

the pattern throughout. Press work on the wrong side, opening the seams out flat.

Place lining fabric over right side of patchwork and join all round, $\frac{1}{2}$ inch from the edge, leaving an opening one side. Turn work out to right side through the opening then sew up opening. Press seams.

If required, enclose some flannel, or an old blanket, between the lining and patchwork. To hold the layers together stabstitch all round seams. See diagram 10 for stab-stitch.

This same idea of joining squares together can be used effectively for cushions, garden cloths or bedspreads.

CRAZY PATCHWORK

For this type of needlework you may use any shapes and sizes available, but you will find it looks better if you arrange the patterned pieces to be separated by plain ones.

Arrange the pieces on a large sheet of brown paper, or on lining material. Try to match the grain of the fabric as much as possible; that is to say, place straight edges to straight and bias ones to bias. This prevents the work puckering afterwards.

Turn in and overlap the edges, then tack in position. Make sure the work is smooth before joining the pieces together with single feather-stitch (see diagram 28a). Press work on wrong side. Remove tacking. Straighten the patchwork edges and line as given for cot cover above.

PATTERNED PATCHWORK

Diagram 62 : 'Star' Motif on a Round Cushion. This motif is built up of a diamond shape which is very easy to assemble. It is a good beginner's piece for learning the basic principles of patchwork.

Diagram 63. Actual-size Diamond Pattern. Trace off the actual-size diamond. Using tracing as a pattern, cut six pieces from brown paper. Place paper template over material and allow $\frac{1}{4}$ inch all round when cutting pieces. Cut six pieces.

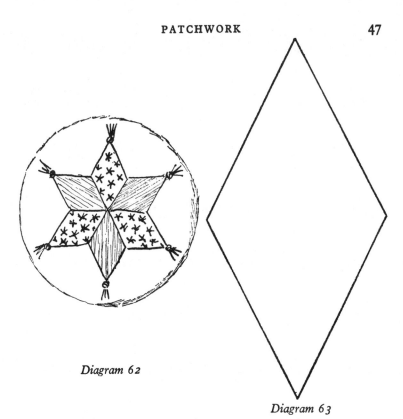

Diagram 62

Diagram 63

Diagram 64. Tack the material over the paper on the wrong side as shown. Tack each piece of material to paper in this way before making up.

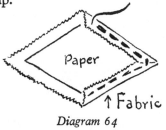

Diagram 64

Diagram 65. Place two pieces together, right sides inside, and oversew the edges together neatly along one facet of diamond shape only. Assemble the remaining pieces in the same way, to form the 'star'. See page 129 for making round cushion, but sew motif to front before making up cushion.

Pin motif in place and hem the edges invisibly (see diagram 8). Remove the paper and tacking-stitches before sewing the final diamond down to the fabric.

Make small tassels of Anchor Soft Embroidery or fine wool and sew one to each point. See page 108 for tassels.

Diagram 65

PATCHWORK TEMPLATES

These are available from needlework shops in varying sizes and shapes. They are used to cut the fabric and paper accurately, thus ensuring a perfect locking together of patterns. Templates may be made from stiff card if required. Some of the more popular shapes are illustrated here.

Diagram 66. (*a*) Hexagon. (*b*) Church Window. (*c*) Triangle.

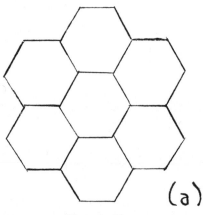

Diagram 66

(d) Box pattern – a different arrangement of the diamond shapes used for the 'star' pattern.

Always try several colour arrangements when putting the pieces together. Try to distribute the colours and patterns evenly.

When decorative stitching is used to cover the seams this should always be worked in a neutral shade throughout.

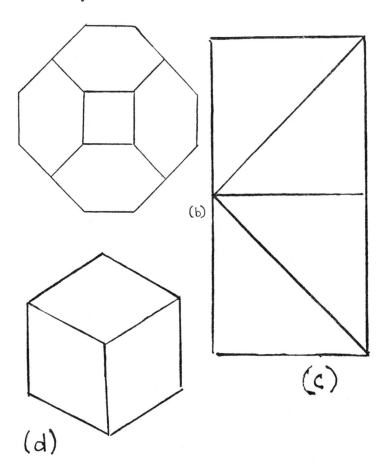

(b)

(c)

(d)

Diagram 66

CHAPTER 6

Quilting

THIS traditional embroidery is both charming and practical. Only the simplest stitching is used to form the decoration and to hold the layers of material together.

There are two distinct types of quilting and each will be dealt with separately as the techniques are also different.

ENGLISH QUILTING

This is the more practical one as it consists of three layers, one of which is padding, and is suitable for bed covers, tea cosies and other insulating articles.

The top layer should be fairly fine silk, satin, taffeta or linen. The lining should be fine muslin or cotton. The padding can be varied, according to the purpose of the articles. For anything which is to be laundered often, domette is suitable. For warmth, layers of cotton wool may be used. For cushion covers, a flannelette or winceyette.

Transfers of traditional quilting designs are available from needlework shops and a selection of these is illustrated opposite for your guidance:

Diagram 67. (*a*) Shell. (*b*) Fan. (*c*) Feather. (*d*) Pine. (*e*) *Fleur-de-lis.* (*f*) Leaf.

It is also quite interesting to make up quilting patterns with geometrical shapes, and a few suggestions are given.

Patterns should be transferred on to the lining and the work done from the wrong side. The reason for this is that the stitching does not form a continuous line and the transfer ink would show between the stitches on the surface.

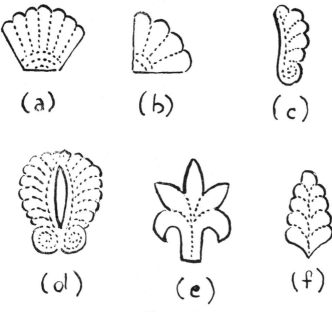

(a)　(b)　(c)

(d)　(e)　(f)

Diagram 67

The design should be worked in the one stitch throughout and the most suitable stitch for holding the three layers together firmly is stab-stitch (see diagram 10). Machine-stitching, with the stitch as long as possible, is also suitable.

The preparation for quilting is most important. This consists of tacking the three layers of material together very carefully. Lay these on a flat surface, lining first, padding next and finally the top layer. Pin the outer edges to keep them in place. Begin tacking through the layers, using a very fine tacking-thread and the stitch shown in diagram 68(*b*) and work from the centre to the outer edge. In this way any bulges can be smoothed out as the work proceeds. Keep the tacking about 1 inch apart in each direction as shown in diagram.

Diagram 68 (*a*) Layers of material tacked together ready for quilting. (*b*) *Tacking*. Run needle in and out of layers, making stitches ¼ inch long and using special tacking thread.

The quilting should be done in the same colour as the top layer material. Sewing cotton is quite suitable, but two strands of embroidery thread may be used if required.

Work the stab-stitch evenly through the three layers, following the line of the design. The purpose of the stitching is to indent the fabric and throw the design into relief.

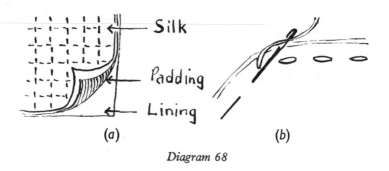

Silk

Padding

Lining

(a)   (b)

Diagram 68

The quilting design should be centralized and the background worked in square or diagonal trellis. It is not advisable to leave large areas unworked as the interlining must be held firmly in position. Do not remove the tacking-threads until all the quilting has been completed. If the wrong side of the work is to be seen (such as on a bed cover), then it should be lined with the same material as the top layer. Articles such as hot-water-bottle covers need not be lined over the muslin.

Quilting is best done on a frame. The most suitable frame is a square one with webbing and tapes to hold the work taut. The layers are sewn to the webbing ready for quilting.

For your first lesson in quilting make a simple pot holder in checked gingham and use cotton wool for the padding.

Diagram 69: Quilted Pot Holder. You will need two 7-inch squares of gingham, a 7-inch square of cotton-wool wadding; 30 inches of bias binding and a small curtain ring; matching sewing-thread.

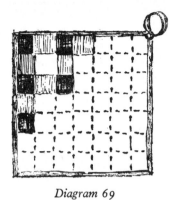

Diagram 69

Place the wadding between the gingham squares and tack the three layers together as shown in diagram 68.

Stab-stitch (see diagram 10) over vertical and horizontal lines, forming 1-inch squares throughout. Bind the edges with bias as shown in diagram 7. Sew ring to one corner. Remove tacking thread.

QUILTED PRAM COVER

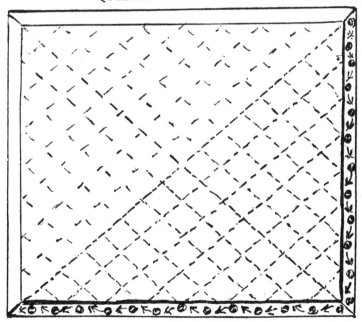

Diagram 70.

Materials: Two pieces of satin, 27 by 23 inches; a piece of domette the same size; 3 yards matching blanket binding;

matching sewing-thread and 3 skeins of Anchor Stranded Cotton – one green and two shades of pink or yellow for embroidery on blanket binding.

Take one piece of satin to mark off for quilting. First rule a 1-inch margin all round the rectangle (this will be enclosed in the binding afterwards). Fold the rectangle from corner to corner in each direction, pressing the fold with a cool iron. Using a ruler, pencil parallel lines 2 inches apart each side of folds until the entire area inside margin is covered, forming a diamond trellis.

Prepare the three layers and work the quilting as explained on page 52.

Pin the blanket binding all round the margin as shown on page 6, allowing 3 inches at each corner for mitring. Tack the folds for the corners and remove binding.

Embroidery: First trace off the actual-size motif given below and transfer it to the centre of ribbon binding with embroidery carbon. Repeat the motif as required.

Diagram 71

Diagram 71: Trace-off motif. Embroider the roses in bullion-stitch (see diagram 19) using the darker shade inside the flower. Work the stalks in stem-stitch (diagram 41) and leaves in lazy-daisy stitch (diagram 34). Press embroidery on wrong side.

Now bind the pram cover as given for blanket on page 5.

ITALIAN QUILTING

This is more decorative than practical, and the padding is restricted to the outlining of the designs. This type of quilting is ideally suited to cushion covers.

Nightdress trimmed with honeycomb smocking *(see page 63)*

Place mat *(see page 8)*

Contemporary rug *(see page 149)*

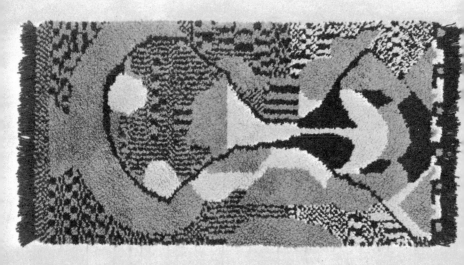

For the top layer use fine silk or satin. The material must be soft to obtain the right effect. No interlining is necessary, but muslin is needed for the backing.

Special 8-ply wool is available for this quilting, but you could also use strands of knitting or embroidery wool to make up the required thickness. The thickness of the padding depends on the width of the double lines – the effect should be that of a raised line on the right side and should not appear too hard, otherwise the design will cockle out of shape.

The design should be drawn on the muslin and must consist of double lines throughout. Small circles and other small shapes may be introduced, but the area to be padded should not exceed about half an inch in any space.

Tack the two layers of material together as given for English Quilting, page 50. Work tiny running-stitches over all the pattern lines, making sure that the needle goes through both layers of material every time. See diagram 6 for running-stitch. The outlines may be machine-stitched if required.

Padding. This is inserted from the wrong side of the work. Use a blunt wool needle to pass the strand through the double lines. When an angle is reached, or when passing a curve, remove the needle and re-insert it again as shown.

Diagram 72: Italian Quilting. Transfers are available for Italian Quilting, but you could first experiment on your own following the suggestions given below.

If you have any material with isolated flower sprays you could use this for the top layer, Using a tumbler for a pattern, encircle the flower spray with double lines. The effect will be that of tiny picture-frames. This would be particularly charming if worked on sprigged organdie, using a wool to match the flower-sprigs for the quilting.

Diagram 72

Diagram 73: Quilting Pattern, for Baby's Crib. Another way to build an interesting pattern would be to take a

simple leaf from the garden and trace the design. The leaf
veining would make ideal 'runways' for the quilting wool.

Diagram 74: Leaf Motif Cushion. Smaller leaves and flower
shapes could also be used, and the petals filled with cotton wool
(if the article is not likely to be washed). To fill the areas open
the muslin and push the cotton wool into the space, smoothing
it out with a blunt needle, then sew up the opening.

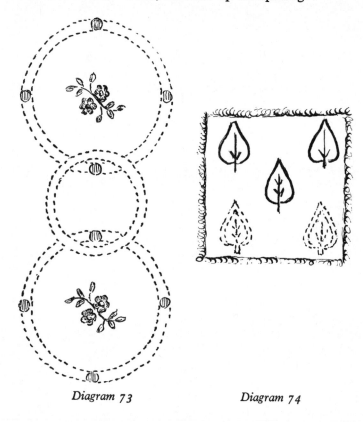

Diagram 73   *Diagram 74*

CHAPTER 7

Smocking

THIS is a favourite form of decoration for children's clothes. Ready-made garments with this trimming are quite expensive and it certainly is an advantage to be able to do the embroidery oneself.

From time to time this technique is introduced into women's clothing too, and when smocking is fashionable it is satisfying to be able to do it to suit individual requirements.

Fine fabric is most suitable for this type of work. Allow three times the width of the smocking when calculating the width of the fabric. Patterned fabrics with spots, checks or stripes can be smocked without transfers.

Transfers are available for smocking. These are in strips of dots, varying from $\frac{1}{8}$ to $\frac{1}{2}$ inch apart, the rows being about $\frac{1}{2}$ inch apart. The wider the space between the dots the more fabric will be needed because of the greater depth of each pleat. The most usual distance for dots is $\frac{1}{4}$ inch. If applying the transfer to a circular yoke, cut up between the vertical rows of dots and open the paper out to fit the shape required. Transfers should be ironed off on to the wrong side of the fabric, following the grain, for the depth required.

Alternatively the rows of dots can be marked on the wrong side of the fabric using a ruler and pencil. The dots should be evenly spaced $\frac{1}{4}$ inch apart and the successive rows marked immediately below these dots, making the rows $\frac{1}{2}$ inch apart.

Use sewing-cotton for the gathering and three or more strands of embroidery thread (according to the thickness of the fabric being used) in a crewel needle for the smocking.

Colours for the embroidery are largely a matter of personal taste, and depend on the fabric being used. The stitching is emphasized if worked in a darker tone of the fabric colour. Several shades of the one colour look effective on plain fabric. If the fabric is of a delicate nature, with perhaps an overcheck or spot in a contrast, then choose the same shade as the contrast for the smocking. On gingham use the colour of the checks, and the white, with one dark contrast. Too many colours look confusing and should be avoided.

The preparation for smocking is most important. It is necessarily slow, but the success of the needlework depends on the evenness of the gathering. This is done on the wrong side. Use a separate thread for each row of gathering, this should be the length of the fabric being gathered. Start with a large knot and a back-stitch to secure the thread at the beginning (see diagram 3 for back-stitch). Pick up a tiny portion of the fabric beneath each dot in turn, and leave the thread hanging loosely at the end of the row. Work each successive row in the same way, immediately under the previous row, keeping the stitches very even throughout. When all the rows have been worked, draw up the gathering threads to the required measurement and tie the threads together two by two to secure the gathers. Even out the gathers and stroke them with the point of your needle to ensure that they are even throughout.

Smocking : This is worked on the right side, each stitch being taken through a pleat formed by the rows of gathering. Use the rows of gathering as a guide to keep the stitching straight. Leave a clear margin all round for seams.

Before starting to embroider, make a plan of the pattern to be worked. It is advisable to work one or two straight rows at the beginning to keep the pleats in place. Count the number of pleats if a stitch involving several pleats is to be used as each side of the smocking must match. For instance, if you wish to work wave-stitch over eight pleats, then the total must be divisible by eight. Leave any extra pleats to be worked in a straight-stitch if necessary; an odd one or two may be left unworked at the extreme edges of panels, providing the pleats are secured by straight rows each side.

Stitches : Diagrams and working instructions are given for the basic stitches. These can be repeated as required to build up borders. Work from left to right and do not pull the working thread too tight as the elasticity will be affected.

Diagram 75: Outline-Stitch. Pick up each successive pleat, bringing the needle out over the working thread each time.

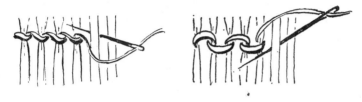

| *Diagram 75* | *Diagram 76* |

Diagram 76: Cable-Stitch. Pick up each successive pleat, but bring the needle out above and below the working thread alternately.

Diagram 77: Wave-Stitch. Work up and down from one row of gathers to another, over successive pleats as shown. Advance over four pleats in each direction. Another row may be worked in reverse to form a trellis pattern. Keep the working thread below the needle when advancing up and above the needle when working down.

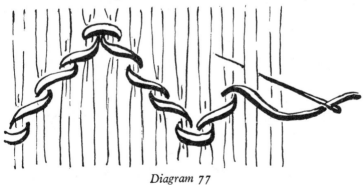

Diagram 77

Diagram 78: Diamond-Stitch. Work from one row of gathers to the other, over two pleats as shown, keeping the thread below the needle when working the two stitches up to the top line and keeping it above the needle when working the two stitches down to the lower line.

Combinations of these stiches are limitless, but some examples are given, including embroidery stitches.

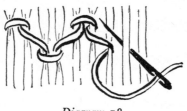

Diagram 78

Diagram 79. Pattern comprising two rows of outline-stitch and four rows of wave-stitch.

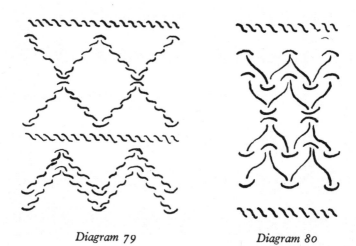

Diagram 79   *Diagram 80*

Diagram 80. Band of outline- and interlaced diamond-stitch.

Diagram 81. Lozenge pattern comprising wave- and cable-titch, with lazy-daisy stitch motifs (see diagram 34).

Diagram 81

Diagram 82. Feather-stitch (diagram 28*a*) and outline-stitch forming tiny hearts with french knot centres (diagram 31).

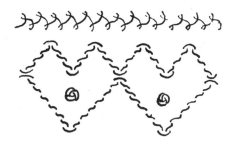

Diagram 82

Finishing: Do not remove the gathering threads before pressing. Do not let the iron rest on the fabric but steam press the pleating from the wrong side of work. Allow the work to dry then remove the gathering threads so that the smocking expands for making up.

Diagram 83: Smocked Apron. This pretty apron would make a welcome gift for a hostess friend. It can be made from ½ yard of 36-inch sheer fabric, with a ½-inch overcheck pattern. You will need 1 yard of 1½-inch-wide matching ribbon for ties, some matching sewing-thread and 1 skein of Anchor Stranded Embroidery.

No pattern is required. Work shell edging all round the piece of fabric.

Diagram 84: Shell Edging. Turn in a narrow hem. Work four tiny running stitches (see diagram 6) along the hem edge, then take the needle over the folded edge twice, drawing the thread up firmly

Diagram 83

to form the shell. Continue in this way throughout.

Work a band of smocking across the 36-inch width about 1-inch from edge. Prepare the work as given on page 58 and pattern in diagram 80 would be quite suitable. Work the rows of gathering through the intersections of the check pattern or use a transfer if required.

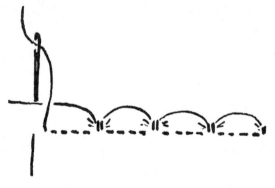

Diagram 84

Sew ribbon ties each side of smocked band.

Many articles may be made from straight pieces of fabric in this way. For a baby's sun dress work two separate pieces to size required. Join sides and leave smocked band open for armholes. Add ribbon straps.

Honeycomb Smocking: This is a simple type of embroidery and takes up less material than ordinary smocking stitches. Only twice the width is required as the stitch has a wide expansion after working. It may be worked without preliminary gathering if suitably patterned fabric is being used, but for a first attempt it will be found easier to have the rows of pleats formed by the gathering.

Diagram 85: Honeycombing. This is worked in double rows so that the stitching can be vandyked from one row to the other and allow for the expansion afterwards. Stitch two pleats together on the first row then take the needle to the second row and stitch together two more pleats (including one from the first pair) as shown. Continue stitching up and down alternately and working two stitches over each pair of pleats.

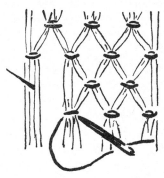

Diagram 85

NIGHTDRESS (see photograph between pages 54 and 55).

No pattern is required for this glamorous nightdress trimmed with honeycomb smocking on the yoke. No transfer will be needed if fabric with a ½-inch spot is used.

This garment is designed to fit a 34-inch bust measurement, but can be adjusted to other sizes if required.

Materials: 2 yards of 36-inch-wide cotton fabric with spots ½ inch apart; 4 yards of ¾-inch-wide lace edging; 1 skein Clark's Anchor Stranded Cotton (for the embroidery); matching sewing-thread.

Cutting Out. First make sure that the fabric has been cut quite straight so that the spot pattern is on the grain of the fabric. Cut off two 1-inch wide strips across width (for straps) then cut the remaining fabric in half across the width for the front and back alike.

Before working the honeycombing, turn in a ¼-inch-wide hem along one cut edge of each section and tack this in position. See diagram 64 for tacking-stitch. Over this hem sew the lace edging, machining this in place or using running-stitch (see diagram 6). This will keep the hem in place. Remove the tacking-thread and press hem.

Embroidery: Work the honeycoming on each section (for the yoke) before making up the nightdress. Leave ½ inch at each selvedge edge and begin the gathering ½ inch from hemmed edge. Prepare the work with six rows of gathering as described for smocking on page 58. Draw the gathered section up to measure 18 inches.

Use three strands of embroidery thread in a crewel needle and work three rows of honeycombing as shown in diagram 85. Press the embroidery as described on page 61, then remove the gathering threads.

Making up: Join the side seams up to the smocking only. Make a ½-inch-wide seam on the machine or back-stitch by hand. See diagram 3 for back-stitch. Each side of smocking turn in the selvedge edge and hem on wrong side. See diagram 8 for hemming. Hem the lower edge and trim with lace edging as given for top edge. Join ends of lace edging neatly. Press seams.

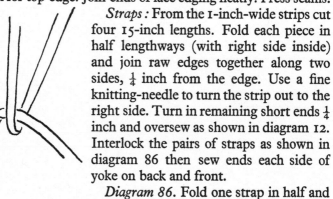

Straps: From the 1-inch-wide strips cut four 15-inch lengths. Fold each piece in half lengthways (with right side inside) and join raw edges together along two sides, ¼ inch from the edge. Use a fine knitting-needle to turn the strip out to the right side. Turn in remaining short ends ¼ inch and oversew as shown in diagram 12. Interlock the pairs of straps as shown in diagram 86 then sew ends each side of yoke on back and front.

Diagram 86. Fold one strap in half and loop other strap through centre as shown.

Diagram 86

CHAPTER 8

Needlework-Tapestry

IT is very expensive, in fact almost impossible, to buy any hand-worked tapestry so it really is a worthwhile hobby. British Queens have worked many exquisite pieces which are a great source of inspiration, and the specimens from past ages prove how well this type of needlework wears.

Needlework-tapestry enhances reproduction furniture and lends atmosphere in modern settings. A single piece of needlework can echo the isolated colours used in a room through the subtle blending of shades.

This type of embroidery is not quick to do, but is a restful and pleasant occupation, particularly in the long winter evenings.

Besides the ever-popular chair coverings, it is used for fire-screens and table-tops. Handbags and spectacle-cases also make beautiful gifts.

Designs: Canvases are available with the design painted in the colours ready for use; you only have to stitch over the crossings of the canvas threads in a corresponding colour. Alternatively the canvas is trammed – that is laid out in long stitches in the specific colours of the design; some designs may have the intricate sections already worked in *petit-point.* Canvases may be prepared to individual requirements by tapestry specialists; to obtain a quotation for this you will need to send a paper pattern of the required size, together with details of the type of design preferred.

Charts are available for working on plain canvas. In this case each symbol in the chart represents one stitch on the canvas and a key is given for the colours.

Those with creative talent will wish to design their own

pieces. One may study old designs in libraries or go to a museum, where one can obtain postcards or photostats of traditional patterns. Such designs may be freely adapted for personal use, but may not be used commercially.

Adapting Designs: If the design is too small for your purpose, this can be enlarged. For instance, if you wish the design to be twice the size it is, rule the design into $\frac{1}{2}$-inch squares, then rule the area to be covered into 1-inch squares and draw the sections in each square. By reversing this procedure the design may be reduced. The size of the squares may be varied according to the size required. If the design is quite small, make the squares $\frac{1}{4}$ inch and if the design is required three times as large, rule the working area into $\frac{3}{4}$-inch squares. Use crayons to colour in the areas on the original tracing to provide a guide for the stitching on the enlarged canvas.

Materials: Use wool for hardwearing articles such as rugs, cushions, seats and stools. Coats' Tapisserie Wool is available by the skein, in a wide range of colours, and is suitable for using singly when working *gros-point*. Background wool is available by the ounce and sufficient should be bought to cover the whole area – 1 ounce should work 8 square inches – because a different dye lot would spoil the effect. Crewel wool should be used two strands at a time for *petit-point*. Silk and cotton may also be used for delicate work, or pieces not subjected to wear and tear, such as pictures, fire-screens, evening bags, etc. The strands can be made up to the thickness required.

Colours: Choose mellow shades for the design and serviceable colours for the background. Bright colours would be out of character for this type of needlework.

Canvas: This is usually 27 inches wide and is available with single threads (for *petit-point*) or double threads (for *gros-point*). The mesh ranges from coarse with 8 threads to one inch to fine with 20 threads to one inch. Gauze is the finest material and has around 38 threads to one inch – this is suitable for miniatures, etc., and the background is not generally filled in. The most popular canvas mesh size has 16 single threads or 10 pairs of threads.

Needles: These have blunt ends and oval eyes for threading the wool easily. Numbers 19 to 23 are suitable for canvas work, but a fine crewel needle should be used for working on gauze. On no account must the needle force the threads apart during working – it should pass easily through the canvas holes.

Frame: It is advisable to use a frame for needlework-tapestry as it helps to keep the canvas square and the stitches even. An upright, square type is best. This has two wooden rollers and two screw sides. The size of the work should not exceed the length of the webbing which is attached to the rollers. Fold the canvas over to sew it to the webbing and use strong thread to attach the selvedge edges to the sides of the frame.

Working Instructions: Keep the selvedges to the sides. Leave $1\frac{1}{2}$ inches unworked canvas all round to facilitate stretching and mounting afterwards. Use short lengths of wool (about 18 inches or less for fine work) and if the wool becomes twisted while working, let the needle hang down and the wool will untwist. Do not break off the wool but use a sharp scissors to cut it.

Complete the motif before working the background. When working the background stagger the stitches, do not work them in blocks. Make every stitch in two movements – keep one hand on top of the frame to pass the needle to the other hand underneath; return the needle with the hand underneath the canvas. Do not pull the working thread tightly.

If working from a chart it helps to mark the chart in sections of ten; this will enable you to calculate the size of the finished design if the canvas mesh is to have 10 stitches to the inch.

Diagram 87

Stitches: It is important to keep all the stitches slanting in the same direction throughout. Various stitches may be combined in the one piece of work – for instance, fine features may be worked in *petit-point* by opening up the double threads.

Diagram 87: Petit-Point. This is worked on single thread canvas from right to left. The needle is taken over one crossing of threads on the front of work and under two crossings of threads to bring it out for the next stitch as shown.

Diagram 88: Gros-Point. This is worked on double thread canvas from right to left. The needle is taken over one crossing of double threads on the front of work and under two crossings of double threads to bring it out for the next stitch as shown. The longer stitch on the wrong side pads the work and make it very suitable for hard wear.

Diagram 88

Diagram 89: Trammé. This thread is laid between the double threads to be covered by *gros-point*. It helps to cover the canvas threads completely and adds extra wear. Work the trammé stitch with the same thread as used for the over-stitching and it will not be necessary to reverse the work for alternate rows.

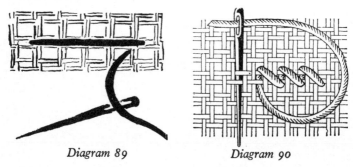

Diagram 89   *Diagram 90*

Diagram 90: Half-Cross-Stitch. This is worked in rows from right to left. It has the same effect as *gros-point* on the front of work but has only small upright stitches on the wrong side. It is not suitable for hard wear. It should be worked over a trammé thread if the canvas is likely to show.

Diagram 91 : Gobelin Stitch. This is worked over two threads in height and only one in width. It is sometimes used for working backgrounds.

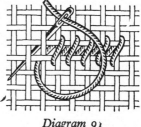

Diagram 91

Diagram 92 : Diagonal-Stitch. This is sometimes used to fill in large areas of background instead of the straight rows. The stitching is done in upward (*a*) and downward (*b*) rows alternately throughout.

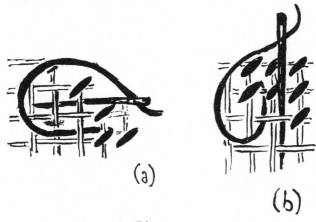

(a)

(b)

Diagram 92

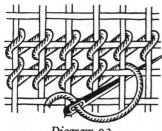

Diagram 93

Diagram 93: Return Rows. These may be worked by turning the canvas and continuing the stitching in the same way, or by working in a contrary direction as shown in diagram.

Diagram 94: Beginning Stitch. Make a knot at the end of the wool and insert the needle through the double crossing of threads a few squares away from where the first stitch is to be made. Bring the needle out in working position and work the first two stitches over the thread lying at the back of work, then cut off the knot.

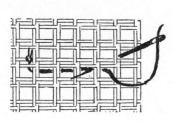

Diagram 94   Diagram 95

To Finish Off Thread: Run the working thread through the back of stitches already worked, then cut off.

Stretching: The character of the stitching is inclined to pull the work to one side, but this can be rectified when the work is complete. Pull the work back into shape carefully and pin it securely to a board, face down. Put the drawing pins in about ¾ inch apart. If the work is laid over squared paper it will be easier to square it off in the pinning process.

Cover the back of the work with damp blotting-paper and leave it under an even weight until completely dry before removing the pins. It may be necessary to repeat this process to get the work absolutely square and ready for mounting.

Mounting: It is well worth having this done professionally for first-class results. Furniture can also be made to fit individual pieces of tapestry. If the mounting is to be done personally, use strong twine to stitch through the edges in each direction as shown in diagram.

Diagram 95: Mounting work. Draw the threads up tightly as each stitch is made and hold the thread taut in the left hand while the next stitch is being worked.

Diagram 96: Rosebud Motif Chart (a). Suitable for an all-over pattern to cover a favourite stool (b).

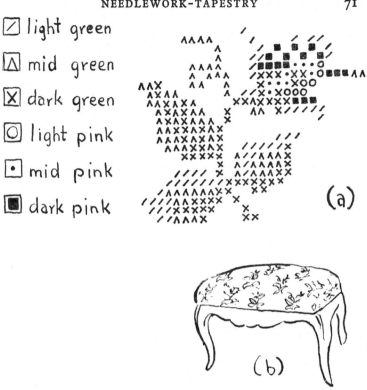

☑ light green

◩ mid green

☒ dark green

◯ light pink

⊡ mid pink

◪ dark pink

(a)

(b)

Diagram 96

COUNTED THREAD EMBROIDERY

This is a very interesting type of needlework. Patterns are worked directly on to the material by counting the threads and following a chart given on squared paper, covering any area required.

There are many suitable fabrics, all of which have an even weave – this means that the threads running lengthways from the cut edge (the warp) and those running across from selvedge to selvedge (the weft) should be of the same thickness. The number of threads to the inch in the fabric governs the finished size of the embroidered design.

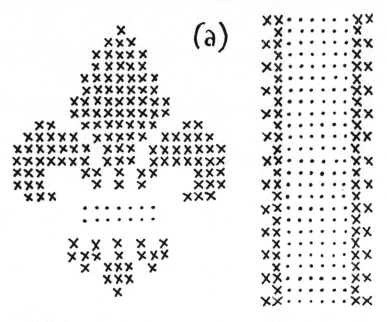

(a)

☒ main colour

⊡ contrast

Diagram 97: Fleur-de-Lis and Ribbon Motif (a). This pattern may be used to cover a treasured antique chair (b) or repeated for cushions. Adaptable to any colour scheme. Work motifs six rows apart, and ribbon three rows away from motif.

(b)

It is most important to use blunt needles for this work, so that the threads are not split, and the needles must have large eyes to pull the thread easily through the fabric.

For fine embroidery use even-weave linen and a No. 21 tapestry needle. Use stranded embroidery thread, using the number of strands equalling the thickness of the fabric weave.

For medium embroidery use bincarette or java cloth and a No. 19 tapestry needle. These fabrics have a squared mesh and holes through which the needle passes easily. Embroidery cotton or perlé is suitable.

For coarse embroidery use canvas or Binca, and a No. 14 tapestry needle. Thick embroidery wool or thread, such as Perlita or Fresca, would be suitable.

Diagram 98: Florentine Pattern. This is best worked on single thread canvas, using several shades of the one colour. It consists of upright stitches, forming vandyke patterns. This example, worked over an even number of threads, is an ideal pattern for a beginner.

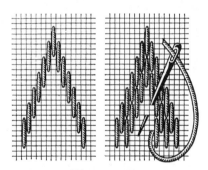

Diagram 98

Diagram 99: Shell Pattern. This is more ambitious and would be very effective if worked for a chair-seat or cushion. Use black for the outline and four shades of rose for the encroaching stitches within the outline. Work the outline pattern over all the area before filling in the remainder. In this way it will be easier to count the pattern.

Diagram 100: Border Pattern. Quick to work on even-weave linen, for place mats, tray-cloths or curtains.

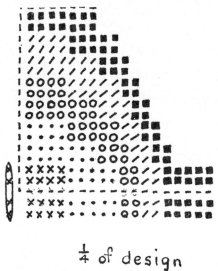

¼ of design

Diagram 99

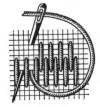

Diagram 100

Part 3

PRACTICAL SEWING

CHAPTER 9

Sewing-Machines

THERE are many types of sewing-machine on the market, but they fall into two categories. One has a fixed needle and the other a swing needle. There is a vast difference in price and you should consider the amount of use the machine will have before making your purchase.

Fixed-Needle Machine. This is the simplest type and quite suitable for the average home sewing. It sews in a straight line and can be fitted with various attachments for hemming, piping and binding, etc. This is the safest machine for the inexperienced dressmaker.

Swing-Needle Machine. This will sew forwards and backwards in the normal way. In addition it will sew sideways, producing zig-zag stitching. This is useful for joining stretchy materials and also for overlocking fraying edges. Practice is necessary to be able to adjust the stitches for sewing on buttons and making buttonholes. Several extra attachments are available and an experienced dressmaker would enjoy using this machine.

Automatic Swing-Needle Machine. This machine is for the expert. It is capable of producing complicated embroidery patterns through the medium of discs and dials. It is essential to learn how to operate this machine properly and a demonstrator should be available.

Instruction Book: Every machine should have one of these handbooks. If the machine is second-hand you should write to the manufacturers for a handbook. Study the handbook before attempting to make a garment. Oil your machine regularly, using the special oil recommended. If there is any point you cannot understand in the handbook call in at a local showroom to ask advice. Alternatively ask a representative to call at your home.

Tension: There are two tensions on the machine. The upper tension controls the thread from the reel and the lower tension controls the thread from the bobbin. The stitch should sink into the fabric equally on each side. If the top thread appears too tight, turn the tension screw to the left. If the bobbin thread is too loose (forming loops round the top thread) then turn the bobbin screw to the right to tighten the tension. Only minor adjustment should be necessary and the discrepancies are sometimes caused by the thickness of the thread.

Stitches: Every machine has a lever for adjusting the length of the stitch. The length should be varied according to the thickness of the fabric being used. For heavy materials, such as coatings, 8 stitches to one inch is suitable, but for sheer fabrics, up to 20 stitches to one inch would give the best results.

Needles: These are also in various sizes, and should be fitted for different thicknesses. A No. 18 needle would be suitable for heavy cloth and a No. 9 for sheer fabrics. The automatic machines can be fitted with twin needles so that different colours may be used for double stitching. Needles must always be quite straight and the points sharp.

Threads: These should be varied with the thickness of fabric. Use size 30 to 40 for heavy materials and 80 to 100 on sheer fabrics. Also, you must use the right type of thread – cotton, silk or nylon, according to the fabric being used.

Machine Sewing. Hold the bulk of the material on the left of the needle and guide the material with your left hand. When sewing darts or angles, stop the machine when the needle is down in the material at the point, then release the pressure foot and turn the material as required. In this way the needle will hold the material in the right position. When sewing is finished, stop the machine when the needle is in a raised position.

Use the longest stitch possible when working gathering or marking.

Diagram 101: Threading the needle. The upper thread should pull from the back of the spool. Place spool on pin above machine and hold spool with the right hand. Pass thread through A fixture, down round tension screw B. Take thread

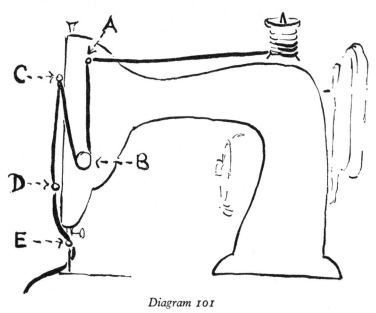

Diagram 101

up to take-up spring C then through regulator D on side of machine and finally through guide E on the needle clamp. Thread the needle from front to back through the eye – place a scrap of plain white paper behind the needle if you have difficulty in threading the eye. Hold the thread and drop the needle down to pick up the bobbin thread, then draw both threads to the back of the machine under the pressure foot.

This procedure may vary according to the make of the machine, but the general principle should be the same.

Test the tension on a piece of paper before sewing the material.

MACHINE EMBROIDERY

Any fixed-needle machine can be guided to achieve charming results with embroidery designs. Machine embroidery is very popular nowadays and is particularly effective on delicate fabrics.

The fabric to be embroidered should be mounted in a hoop frame, with the right side inside (so that the fabric will be flat on the surface when being enbroidered). The frame keeps the fabric taut and it is easier to move around so that the needle can follow the pattern. If the fabric is very delicate, tack some paper to the wrong side to give it body while stitching. The paper is easily removed afterwards.

In some embroideries thicker threads may be used in the needle to give a three-dimensional quality to the work. If this is done, be sure to use a larger needle in the machine.

Before using the machine, remove the foot and cover the teeth below the foot (a special plate is available for this). Keep the pressure lever down throughout the stitching.

Work the continuous lines first, then the shading effects can be obtained with rows of stitching close together for solid contrast. When moving from one part of the design to another cut off the threads close to the background. Handle the machine skilfully to keep the outlines as clear as possible.

The automatic machine can produce embroidery stitches. It is possible, if one has such a machine, to work monograms and also to do *appliqué* and cutwork. The swing needle moves to work the embroidery stitches, instead of having to move the fabric as with a fixed needle machine.

FLOWER PICTURE (see photograph between pages 86 and 87).

This study of meconopsis (blue poppy) looks most effective. It was sewn on a fixed-needle machine with the addition of a few embroidery stitches.

The flowers are in three shades of blue, the leaves in dark green and the buds in dark brown – all taffeta scraps, applied to a grey background by machine.

Diagram 102

In addition to the pieces mentioned above, you will need some small pieces of blue, black and beige nylon net or gauze (for the shadows). Also a few dark beads for the flower-centres.

Use dark blue and light green sewing-thread for machining and three strands of matching embroidery thread for the hand embroidery. Also a length of white embroidery thread for the stamens in one flower.

Diagram 102: Reduced Flower Study Design. Trace off the design as given, then rule the tracing up to $\frac{3}{8}$-inch squares. Enlarge the design by drawing $1\frac{1}{8}$-inch squares on another sheet and drawing in the corresponding shapes.

Transfer the outline of the enlarged design to the background fabric, using embroidery carbon.

Use the enlarged tracing as a pattern, and the photograph as a guide to light and dark shade shapes, to cut out the various pieces of taffeta. Tack each piece in position on the background design, then tack net shapes over the design as shown.

With corresponding colours machine-stitch three or four rows inside and outside the design edge. Also machine over some of the leaf and petal markings. Machine several rows close together for the stalks.

Carefully cut away the net from over the light petals of design.

Embroidery: Work petal markings in stem-stitch (see diagram 41) and french knots (diagram 31) for bud markings. Outline all the stalks with buttonhole-stitch (diagram 20), keeping the purl edge against the edge of the stalk. Sew beads to each flower-centre and embroider the seeds in top poppy centre in lazy-daisy stitch (see diagram 34).

Finally catch down the net shapes to the background as invisibly as possible where it is not caught in by machining. Press embroidery well on the wrong side.

Simple flower-shapes skeletonized in machine-stitching look charming on table-mats. Nursery motifs can be worked in the same way on baby clothes.

Dressmaking

THE world of fashion opens up to you if you can sew well. It is less expensive to make clothes and you can choose the most becoming lines and colours, also ensure perfect fit.

Dressmaking skill comes with practice so you must have patience in the beginning and do everything in easy stages.

Tools: These are not expensive. You will need a 60-inch linen tape measure and a small ruler for making darts, etc. Cutting shears should be about 8 inches long, and you should have a small pair of scissors (about 5 inches) with sharp points for cutting buttonholes and for snipping curves. A pair of pinking shears is useful for notching seams to prevent fraying. Thimble must fit the second finger well and should be steel lined. You will need plenty of steel pins – they will not mark the fabric.

It is essential to have an efficient iron and a flannel-lined ironing-board. Make yourself a pressing-pad from flannel filled with cotton wool – this is useful for pressing curved seams.

Make a working pin-cushion by twisting some flannel round the body of the sewing-machine. A wrist pin-cushion may be made from folded flannel attached to elastic.

Tailor's chalk should be used for marking lines on fabrics. This is available in tablet form.

Fabrics: You will get the best results from good firmly woven fabrics. Make sure that the colour suits you by looking at the fabric in the daylight first.

Pattern scale is also most important. If you are small, fine fabrics with small or vertical striped designs are most suitable. For the tall figure choose bulky tweeds or shaggy woollen fabrics with bold patterns. For large figures it is best to choose fine fabric with very neat checks or vertical stripes.

Amounts are generally quoted on the pattern envelope and if the fabric chosen has a nap or pattern to match, more fabric may be needed.

Woollen cloth is usually 54 inches wide, folded with the right side inside, and cottons are 36 inches wide, folded right side out.

For a first attempt at dressmaking choose a plain fabric, or one with an all-over reversible pattern such as gingham, which is easy to match.

Sizes: Take your measurements accurately and the size will be right. Take the measurements over a slip and a foundation garment, and do not pull the tape tightly. *Bust:* Measure around the body and place the tape measure over the fullest part of the bust. *Waist:* Around the natural waistline, holding tape measure firmly. *Hips:* Measure around the fullest part, usually about 7 inches below the waistline.

Mark down your measurements and these can be referred to when you are selecting paper patterns. For dresses choose the bust size and adapt the hips or waist if necessary. For skirts, choose the hip measurement and adapt waist if necessary.

Ease is allowed for in the pattern sizing, so buy according to your actual measurements.

Patterns: If you are a beginner, choose a simple style, preferably one without a waist seam and without collar or sleeves.

Know your figure and choose accordingly. If you are short, unbelted styles will give height. Also, avoid fussy collars and choose short jacket styles. For the tall figure, long-line jackets and slightly flaring skirts look best. For the large figure, simple tailored styles are most flattering, also 'V' or open necklines.

Special patterns are available for the short or tall figures. Also there is a range for misses – these are cut slightly smaller than for the women's sizes.

Adjusting Patterns: It is best to fit patterns individually because no two figures are exactly alike. Make alterations on the paper pattern and each pattern will include diagrams on adjustments for the particular style.

Press paper pattern then pin sections together for fitting. To lengthen the pattern cut across wherever it seems to be too short and insert tissue paper to widen the section. Remember to make the same adjustment on both back and front sections. To shorten patterns, pleat across the width for the amount of decrease required. To widen patterns, cut through the pattern vertically and insert tissue paper for the amount of increase required. Adjust waist measurement in the darts – unless the alteration is more than $\frac{1}{4}$ inch in each dart, in which case alter the side seams. To enlarge or decrease hip measurement, make allowance in the side seams (remembering to divide the amount being adjusted by four). Alter sleeves in the centre of pattern for width or above and below elbow for length.

Cutting Out: This must be done on a large flat surface, preferably non-slip and quite hard.

If the selvedge is woven more tightly than the fabric remove it before cutting out. Check that the fabric has been cut quite straight – to do this, pull out a crosswise thread.

Fabrics hang better down the length, so try to cut all the main pieces this way. Follow the pattern layouts for placing the pieces and see that they all fit before cutting out. If you are matching the design you may run a little short of fabric and adjustments can be made for this in the hem allowance or sleeve length, if necessary.

First make sure of the grain of the fabric. Sometimes fabrics have to be pulled diagonally to straighten this. Fabric must be folded on the straight, unless otherwise stated. Fabric with large motif designs must be carefully studied before cutting out. Plan the motifs to appear in the right places when the garment is made up – avoid centralizing large motifs on the bust or in the wrong places on the skirt.

Arrange the pile to face downwards if cutting shaggy fabrics, or upwards if cutting velvet.

Press out creases before cutting out. Do not remove paper pattern as each section is cut out. Leave it pinned until the sections are needed for making up. Cut the notches outside seam as shown.

Diagram 103. Notches cut in fabric to correspond with paper pattern. Cut facings to shape of armhole or neck as shown.

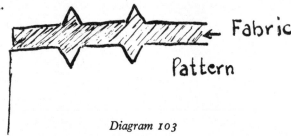

Diagram 103

Diagram 104. Facings. Use tailor's chalk to mark darts, etc.

Bias. Fold material diagonally, so that the lengthwise and crosswise threads meet on the straight, then cut bias from the fold. Bias cut allows the material to give where necessary.

Needles and Threads: For general purposes, size 7 needle is suitable. Crewel needles, with large eyes for easier threading, may also be used. Use size 40 or 50 sewing-cotton for hand and machine-sewing of cotton and rayon fabrics. Pure silk should be used for silk and woollen fabrics. Special buttonhole twist should be used for buttonholes. For tacking or basting, use the special cotton which is very fine and will not mark the fabric; this should be in a contrast colour. For the actual sewing select a thread that is darker than the fabric and thread the needle from the reel (not from the cut end).

Diagram 104

Sewing: It is possible to sew small garments entirely by hand, but it is more convenient to make large garments on a machine.

If sewing by hand, back-stitch (with about 10 stitches to 1 inch) is equivalent to machine stitching. Seams should be machined in the one direction throughout.

Follow the step-by-step instructions included in patterns for making up. Plain seams are intended unless otherwise stated. To make a plain seam place the edges level, with right sides inside, and work back-stitch (or machine-stitch) $\frac{1}{2}$ inch from the edge. Check the pattern for the seam allowance.

Sew darts from the widest part to the point. When assembling gathering, place the gathered section on top of the plain section. Work two rows of gathering for easiest handling.

Clip the curved edges up to $\frac{1}{8}$ inch of the seam so that the seams will lie flat. Fraying edges should be overcast by winding the threaded needle over the edge. Non-fraying fabrics may be pinked with the special shears. Alternatively turn in $\frac{1}{8}$ inch and machine-stitch.

To prevent stretching of curves during fitting and assembly, machine all round inside the seam allowance and following the edge of the curves.

To keep facings in place stitch the inside facing to the double fabric of the seam allowance just inside the seam.

Hems: Fabric is folded twice to enclose the raw edge. Stitches must not show on the right side therefore only one or two threads must be picked up from the main fabric when sewing.

Diagram 105: Catch-Stitch Hem. Fold back $\frac{1}{4}$ inch of tacked hem. Take up one thread on garment, then insert needle through underside of turned-in hem as shown. Do not draw thread tightly.

Diagram 105

Diagram 106: Slip-Stitch Hem. Pick up a single thread on garment, then insert needle through folded edge of hem for $\frac{1}{4}$ inch before bringing it out for next stitch.

Diagram 107: Herringboned Hem. This is suitable for heavy

Diagram 106

coatings which are not too liable to fray. Work herringbone-stitch (see diagram 32) just over the edge and well into the turned fabric as shown.

Lead weights and chains are available in various weights for hems. These are generally encased in fine cloth and sewn in position.

Heavy fabrics are sometimes bound with a bias strip on the inside of hem instead of the double turn.

Bias Binding: This is cut from a diagonal fold and joined along the crossway grain as shown in diagram below.

Diagram 107

Diagram 108: Bias Cutting (a) and Joining (b).

Wide hems should be hand-sewn but some narrow hems may be made on the machine with the relevant attachment.

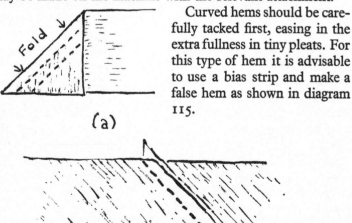

Curved hems should be carefully tacked first, easing in the extra fullness in tiny pleats. For this type of hem it is advisable to use a bias strip and make a false hem as shown in diagram 115.

Diagram 108

Machine embroidered flower picture, piped cushion and motif crochet cushion *(see page 177)*

Bracket light shade, fluted shade and oval shade *(see page 141)*

Tricot blanket *(see page 180)*

Crochet motif *(see page 178)*

Boy's jumper and girl's cardigan *(see pages 164 and 166)*

Lady's cardigan and man's sweater *(see pages 167 and 168)*

Toddler's shift dress *(see page 89)*

Diagram 109: French Seam. This is suitable for garments requiring frequent laundering. Stitch first seam on the right side, $\frac{1}{4}$ inch outside the finished seamline. Trim the seam to $\frac{1}{8}$ inch and press the seam to the edge, on the wrong side. Stitch seam on the wrong side.

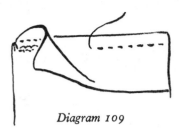

Diagram 109

Diagram 110: Run and Fell Seam. This is ideal for reinforcing where strain occurs. Make seam on right side. Trim lower edge to $\frac{1}{4}$ inch. Turn top fabric in $\frac{1}{8}$ inch and hem, encasing the turnings.

Gathering: This is done with a row of running-stitches (see diagram 6).

Shirring: This consists of several rows of gathering worked close together. Do not draw up the gathering until all the rows have been sewn. If shirring by machine, loosen the tension of the upper thread and lengthen the stitch to the fullest extent.

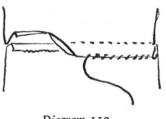

Diagram 110

Pressing: Test for heat on a spare piece of the fabric being used. A very cool iron is required for man-made fibres. A moist cloth, such as a double layer of muslin, must be used for pressing woollen fabrics. Stop pressing when the fabric is still steaming to prevent a shiny appearance. Do not use moisture when pressing silk as this would leave a mark.

Press each seam as it is sewn. Shrink out fullness by using a wet cloth and a hot iron. When pressing pleats or tucks place folded paper under the edge to prevent indenting the fabric underneath.

Velvets must not be pressed. If this is creased hold it over a steaming kettle. Press seams open with fingers or pass these over an inverted steaming iron.

Always press fabric on the wrong side and remove tacking-threads before pressing.

Diagram 111: Tailor's Buttonhole. Mark and cut button-hole, using sharp scissors. The buttonhole should be large enough for the button to pass through freely. Oversew the edges with sewing thread to prevent fraying. With buttonhole twist work the knotted buttonhole stitch as shown in diagram (*a*) along the lower edge. Oversew the corner in a half circle then continue buttonhole stitch along upper edge. Work the

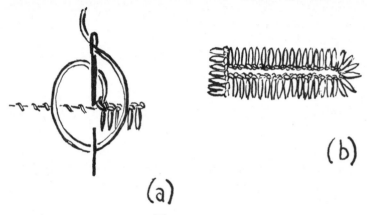

(b)

(a)

Diagram 111

buttonhole stitch in a straight line at the edge of the button-hole as shown in diagram (*b*).

Diagram 112: Bound Buttonhole. Mark and cut buttonhole.

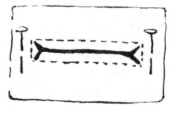

(a)

Cut a binding piece 1 inch longer than buttonhole and about 3 inches wide. Use inter-facing on the wrong side of buttonhole. Pin binding to right side and mark buttonhole position. Stitch $\frac{1}{8}$ inch each side of marking then cut as shown in (*a*). Pull binding through to wrong side and press (b), then sew to interfacing over seam on right side (c). Finally cut the facing, turn in raw edges and slip-stitch over binding (d).

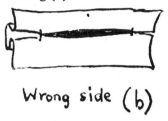

Wrong side (b)

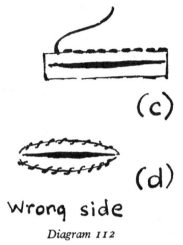

(c)

Buttons : Use button thread for sewing if the garment is to be hard-wearing. The thicker the cloth, the longer the shank should be. If sewing buttons to coats, use interfacing on the inside and connect the stitching to a small button

(d)

Wrong side

Diagram 112

on the inside. Sew button on first, leaving sufficient thread to pass through thickness of fabric, then wind thread around the stem several times before fastening off. Buttons can be covered professionally in chosen materials.

Once the general principles of dressmaking are understood, it will be possible to select any pattern, but some beginners' garments are given here.

TODDLER'S SHIFT DRESS

Diagram 113. This simple dress is quick and easy to make and will fit up to an 18-month-old girl. It buttons through at the back and is trimmed with *Broderie Anglaise* frilling.

Materials : 1 yard 36-inch wide cotton fabric; 1½ yards of 2-inch-wide *Broderie Anglaise* frilling; 4 buttons; matching sewing-thread and bias binding.

Measurements : To fit up to a 22-inch chest measurement; length, 15 inches.

Diagram 114: Shift Dress Diagram.

First make pattern. Use 1-inch squared paper or fold plain paper into 1-inch squares. Draw in the pattern as shown in

diagram 114 which has corresponding squares. Cut out the pattern.

Cutting Out: (see page 83). Cut front section in one piece, placing the indicated line to the fold in the fabric. Cut two pieces for the back, including the facing extensions in pattern. Remember to reverse the paper pattern if the fabric has a right and a wrong side.

Making Up: Join shoulders and sides together with a plain seam (see page 85). Press seams. Fold in extensions on back sections for 1½ inches, then turn under ½ inch and slip-stitch as shown in diagram 106. Press hem.

Diagram 115: Facing with Bias. Place raw edge of bias to raw edge of fabric (with right sides inside) and sew

Diagram 113

together with running-stitch (see diagram 6) along the bias fold line (or ¼ inch from edge). Clip the curved edge (*a*). Turn bias to wrong side, with the seam along the edge, and slip-stitch in position along the folded edge (*b*).

Face the neck and armholes with bias as shown in diagram 115. Turn in ends of bias and oversew (see diagram 12). Press facings. Turn in ½ inch around lower edge, turn under ¼ inch and slip stitch hem. Press hem.

Make four buttonholes on left back section as indicated by

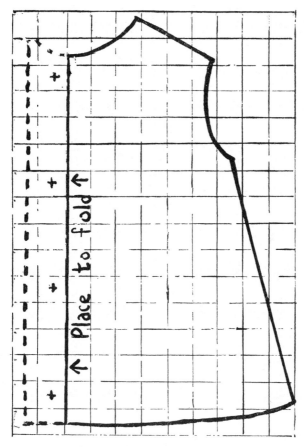

Place to fold

Diagram 114

small cross in diagram. See diagram 111 for tailor's buttonhole. Sew the buttons in corresponding position on right back.

Frill. Narrowly hem short end of *Broderie Anglaise.* Work two rows of gathering along top edge and draw up to fit lower edge of dress. Distribute the gathers evenly then neatly hem the lower edge of dress over the gathering thread. See diagram 8 for plain hemming.

Note. As this shape is so very straightforward it could easily

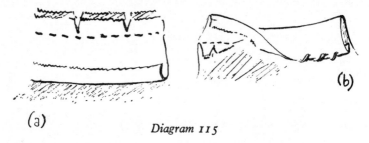

Diagram 115

be adapted to larger sizes. Mark required measurements on the squared paper and try on the pattern before attempting the cutting out.

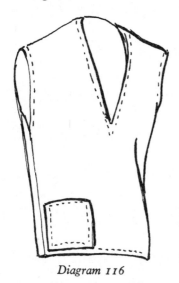

Diagram 116

CORDUROY JERKIN

Diagram 116. This useful garment could be made from a sale remnant. It is fully lined to obviate facings and hems.

Materials: ¾ yard 48- or 54-inch wide corduroy fabric; the same amount of lining; matching sewing-thread.

Measurements: To fit a 36-inch bust measurement (easily adaptable to other sizes by decreasing or increasing the width and length); length, 24 inches.

Diagram 117: Jerkin pattern. First make the pattern. Use 1-inch squared paper or fold plain paper into 1-inch squares. Draw in the pattern as shown in diagram 117, which has corresponding squares. Cut out the pattern.

Cutting Out (see page 83). Cut out back section first placing centre line to straight fold in fabric. Fold pattern along the 'V' neck shape and cut front section, placing the centre line to fold. Cut lining the same.

Making Up: Place the back section and back lining together, with the right side of fabric inside. Join neck edge and armhole edge together with a plain seam (see page 85). Clip seam. Turn out to right side and press seam along edge. Join front section to lining in the same way, but snip centre neck edge up to stitching line before turning out to right side and pressing.

Join side and shoulder seams of corduroy on wrong side and press seams open. Turn in lining $\frac{1}{2}$ inch at shoulders and oversew together over seam (see diagram 12 for oversewing). Join side seams of lining and press. At lower edge turn in $\frac{1}{2}$ inch on corduroy and lining and oversew edges together. Press all seams on wrong side.

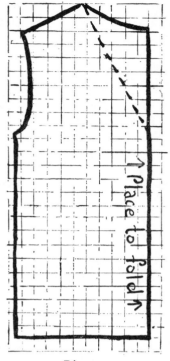

Diagram 117

Work a row of stab-stitch $\frac{1}{2}$ inch from armhole, neck and lower edge (see diagram 10).

Pocket: Cut corduroy and lining 6 inches square. Join together $\frac{1}{2}$ inch from edge on wrong side, leaving an opening. Turn out to right side through opening, then oversew opening. Work stab-stitch $\frac{1}{2}$ inch from one edge (for top of pocket). Pin pocket in required position and stab-stitch to garment $\frac{1}{2}$ inch from edge on remaining three sides.

Note. This pattern could easily be adapted to a shift dress style, by simply extending the pattern lines for length of dress.

BABY'S BIKINI

This useful garment is made from cotton with towelling lining. The edges are quickly bound with bias and the back is elasticated for a snug fit. It opens out flat and fastens with buttons and loops.

Diagram 118

Diagram 118.

Materials: Two bikinis can be made from ½ yard each of cotton fabric and towelling. You will also need ¼ yard of 1-inch-wide elastic, two buttons and 1¼ yards of bias binding for each bikini. Matching sewing-thread.

Measurements: To fit from 1- to 2-year-olds.

Diagram 119: Bikini Pattern. First make the pattern. Use 1-inch squared paper or fold plain paper into 1-inch squares. Draw in the pattern as shown in diagram 119, which has corresponding squares. Cut out the pattern.

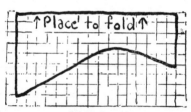

Diagram 119

Cutting Out (see page 83). Cut out towelling and cotton fabric, placing centre line to straight fold in fabrics.

Making Up: First make hem for elastic along wide straight edge. Place cotton over towelling, right sides inside, and join top edge with a plain seam (see page 85). Turn out to right side and stitch 1 inch below through both layers. Thread elastic through this hem and stitch each end securely each side.

Bind the remaining three edges together with bias as described for traycloth on page 3. Make a loop of bias by oversewing (see diagram 12) ends and sides and sew one loop to each corner of top front edge. Sew buttons to back in required position.

CHAPTER 11

Accessories and Trimmings

ADD glamour to everyday clothes with exciting accessories, made from small pieces of luxury fabric.

This type of thing is quite expensive to buy and only a small amount of sewing is involved in the making.

FUR FABRIC BERET AND CRAVAT (see photograph between pages 118 and 119).

This luxurious-looking twosome is simple to make and economical too – only ¼ yard of fur fabric and lining is needed. Fur fabric is available in a wide range of exciting patterns, realistically like mink, lamb, otter, etc., and you may like to make more than one set for your wardrobe.

Materials: ¼ yard Katmandu fur fabric, ⅝ yard satin lining; ⅝ yard 1-inch wide elastic; 1½ in. shank button; matching sewing-thread; vilene for interlining.

Size: To fit a 22-inch head measurement, but easily adaptable to smaller or larger sizes by adjusting the band to fit.

Diagram 120: Beret Pattern. First make the pattern. Use 1-inch squared paper or fold plain paper into 1-inch squares. Draw in the pattern as shown in diagram 120, which has corresponding squares. Cut out the pattern.

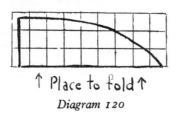

↑ Place to fold ↑

Diagram 120

Cutting Out: Beret. The fur fabric must stroke downwards so all the pieces must be cut the same way (with the pile running from top of beret to base). It is easier to cut fur fabric from the wrong side, so fold the fabric with the right side inside and place the pattern fold line to the straight fold. Cut five pieces alike, immediately under one another, across the fabric. *Cravat.* From remaining fur fabric cut two strips $4\frac{1}{2}$ by 17 inches. From lining and vilene cut exactly the same, plus a strip 3 by 23 inches (for band) and a circle $3\frac{1}{4}$ inches in diameter (for covering button).

Making Up. First tack vilene to wrong side of each fur fabric piece. Place two pieces of fur fabric together, with right sides inside. Join together along one curved edge from top to lower edge with a plain seam (see page 85) $\frac{1}{4}$ inch from edge. Join on remaining pieces in the same way. *Lining.* Make up pieces in the same way, but do not join final edges together. Press lining seams. Place lining over fur fabric shape, with the wrong sides inside and catch-stitch lining seams to fur fabric seams all round. Finally fold in remaining edge of lining and slip-stitch (see diagram 106). Turn out to right side. Stroke seams with a pin to release caught-in pile.

Run a gathering thread along lower edge and draw each section up to measure $4\frac{3}{8}$ inches along the straight edge.

Band: Join short ends of satin and vilene together on the wrong side $\frac{1}{2}$ inch from edge to form a circle. Place right side of band to right side of fur fabric, raw edges together and join $\frac{1}{2}$ inch from edge. Join elastic into a circle to fit head measurement. Turn in $\frac{1}{2}$ inch along other edge of band, then fold band in half, enclosing the elastic the other side of the seam. Hem folded edge of band over seam (see diagram 8).

Button: Place vilene on wrong side of satin and gather all round, through both layers, $\frac{1}{4}$ inch from edge. Place over button and draw up tightly then fasten off securely. Sew button to top of beret.

Cravat: First tack vilene to wrong side of each fur fabric strip. Place the strips of fur fabric together, with the right side inside, and the pile lying the one way. Join along one short edge with a plain seam, $\frac{1}{4}$ inch from edge. Place satin lining over fur fabric, right sides inside, and join both long sides together in the same way. Turn out to right side. Trim ends thus: Place strip on a flat surface, with lining uppermost. On left edge, fold the top edge down 2 inches, forming a diagonal fold to the corner. Cut along fold. Turn the cravat around to the left and trim the other end in the same way.

Turn in raw edges and slip stitch lining over fur fabric.

Strap: Cut lining 1½ by 5 inches. Fold in half lengthways, with right side inside and join long edges together ¼ inch from edge. Turn out to right side and press seam. Sew this strap to the wrong side of right end of cravat, at an angle 2 inches from shaped edge and 6 inches from point, turning in the ends of strap diagonally before stitching. Stroke seams to release caught-in pile.

The cravat is looped through this strap to hold it in position.

FUR HOOD (see photograph between pages 118 and 119).

This cosy hood was made from 'seal' fur fabric and lined with emerald satin. The idea could be copied in jersey fabric for sailing.

Materials: A piece of Lister's fur fabric 13 by 32 inches (with the pile running across the 13-inch width); satin lining the same size; a fur hook (for fastening chin-strap); matching sewing-thread.

Diagram 121: Hood Pattern. First make the pattern. Use 1-inch squared paper or fold plain paper into 1-inch squares. Draw in the pattern as shown in diagram 121, which has corresponding squares. Cut out the pattern.

Cutting Out: The fur fabric must lie from front to back on both sections. Place the front curved edge to the top of fur fabric and turn the pattern upside-down for cutting the second piece as shown.

Diagram 122: Cutting Plan. Cut lining pieces in the same way.

Making Up: First make darts at lower neck edge. Each dart should be 2½ inches long and tapering from 1 inch at lower edge to point. Sew dart on wrong side and cut open through fold to lie flat.

Place fur fabric sections together, right side inside, and join

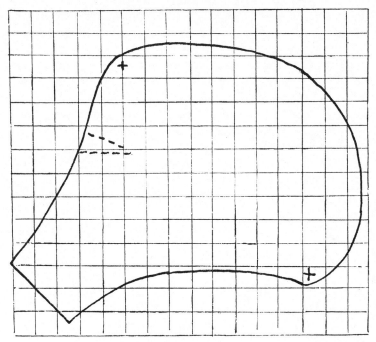

Diagram 121

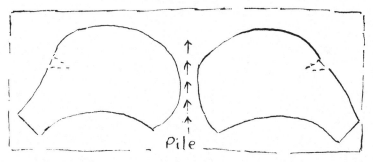

Diagram 122

together along top and back edge (between 'X's) with a plain seam (see page 85). Clip curved edges up to ⅛ inch of stitching, and open seams flat.

Make up lining in the same way and press seams. Place

lining over fur fabric, with the wrong sides inside and catch-stitch lining seam to the fur fabric seam.

Clip the curves at front and lower edges and turn in $\frac{1}{2}$ inch to wrong side, on fur fabric section. On lining clip edges and turn in $\frac{3}{4}$ inch. Slip-stitch lining to fur fabric all round. See diagram 106 for slip-stitch. Press seams.

Sew fur hook to centre of straight section to fasten under chin.

Turn out to right side and stroke the seams with a pin to release caught-in pile.

Diagram 123

BAGS

These are indispensable for every occasion and it is possible to ring the changes with these if they are made quickly and inexpensively.

Diagram 123. It is possible to buy delicate little frames, in silver or gilt finish, with ready-punched holes for attaching fabric.

Instructions are given for making a bag on a 7-inch frame. You will need a piece of brocade or rich satin, 10 by 12 inches, lining and interlining the same measurement. Matching sewing-thread. Also a small packet of matching beads.

Making Up: Place lining over brocade (right sides inside) and cover with interlining. Join the three layers together all round with running-stitch $\frac{1}{2}$ inch from the edge, leaving an opening one side. See diagram 6 for running-stitch. Turn out to right side through opening. Oversew (see diagram 12) opening and press seam.

Fold in half across width, with right side inside, then oversew the sides together from fold up to 2 inches (or depth of frame) from the top edge. Turn out to right side.

Now sew fabric to frame stitching through fabric ⅛ inch from the edge. Begin with sides. Bring needle through hole in frame, through fabric and then through a bead and return needle through the same hole. When sewing the top edge ease the fullness in between stitches to give the effect of tiny tucks.

If required, small pockets for mirror or lipstick may be added to lining before the sides are seamed.

DAY BAG

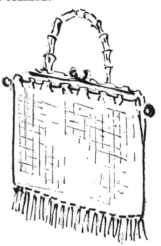

Diagram 124. Large or small metal frames with bamboo handles are available nowadays. These have metal rails with screw knobs and it is possible to interchange the fabric very quickly – the rail is threaded through a hem.

Instructions are given for making a day bag on a frame of this type, measuring 9 inches.

Materials: Two pieces of loosely woven woollen cloth (suitable for fringing), each 12 by

Diagram 124

14 inches; lining and interlining 12 by 18 inches; matching sewing-thread.

Making Up: Place pieces of woollen fabric together, with wrong side inside and machine- or back-stitch (see diagram 3) the pieces together 2 inches from one 12 inch edge (for lower edge). Draw away the crossway threads and trim fringe.

Place lining over woollen fabric, 3 inches from each end (with right side inside). Place interlining over this and sew the three layers together with a plain seam (see page 85), leaving ends open. Turn out to right side. Press seams. Turn in seam allowance on unsewn sides and herringbone (see diagram 107).

At each end turn in $2\frac{1}{2}$ inches to wrong side and machine- or back-stitch 1 inch from edge. Turn under $\frac{1}{2}$ inch and hem over lining. See diagram 8 for hemming. Press hems.

Fold fabric in half (right side inside) and oversew the side edges together securely up to $3\frac{1}{2}$ inches (or depth of frame) from the top edge. Turn out to right side.

Thread rails through hem below the frill and fix to frame.

Diagram 125

BEACH BAG

Diagram 125. This type of bag is most useful on holiday and should be lined with plastic (for carrying swimsuits and towels, etc.).

Materials: A piece of coarse linen 15 by 22 inches and two 8-inch circles of the same fabric; linen backed plastic for lining in the same sizes; $1\frac{1}{4}$ yards of 1-inch -wide fancy braid; $1\frac{1}{2}$ yards of thick cord; 7 curtain rings (about 1-inch size); matching sewing-thread and a 7-inch circle of strong cardboard (for base).

Making Up: First sew two rows of braid to right side of linen, the first one 2 inches from lower (22-inch) edge and the second 2 inches away from first. Attach these with running-stitch (see diagram 6) inside each edge if the braid is flat. If it is textured, hem both sides (see diagram 8).

Clip all along lower edge and join this edge to one circle of fabric with back-stitch (see diagram 3) as shown, $\frac{1}{2}$ inch from edge.

Diagram 126. When sewing a straight edge to a curved one the straight edge must be clipped to within $\frac{1}{8}$ inch of the stitching line to make it lie flat. The amount of clipping depends on the angle of the curve, but generally it is necessary about every inch.

Join sides together with a plain seam (see page 85). Press seam. Now place card over base and cover with remaining circle of linen; turn in edge all round and hem over seam.

Make up lining, omitting card. Place lining over bag shape, with wrong sides inside. Turn in top edge 1 inch, turn under $\frac{1}{4}$ inch and hem folded edge over lining.

Turn out to right side. Sew curtain rings to right side, 1 inch from top edge and 3 inches apart. Thread cord through rings, knot ends.

The size of this bag may be varied considerably as required,

Diagram 126

and would make an excellent carrier for football and other sports gear.

WORK BAG

Diagram 127. You can make a roomy bag for knitting or sewing using a remnant of cretonne and attaching this to the rails of coat hangers, minus the hooks. Slip the ends of fabric through the rail and hem on the wrong side, then join sides up to 3 inches from rail.

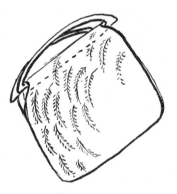

Diagram 127

Alternatively, wooden handles are available for this type of bag.

TRIMMINGS

These can make a lot of difference to the price of bought articles, yet it is a simple matter to add trimmings yourself.

Several ideas are included here for enhancing plain garments and linens, and you will be able to elaborate on them for individual needs.

Fur: Several types of fur, natural or man-made, can be bought by the yard, ready mounted for use. It is available in several colours and varying widths.

Bands of smooth fur may be added to the sleeves of a woollen dress (see diagram 128) or shaggy fur added to coat sleeves and collars.

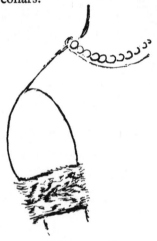

Diagram 128

Diagram 128. Sleeve trimmed with fur.

Lace: Dainty frills of lace can transform a plain knitted garment into a boutique luxury.

Diagram 129. Knitted yoke of matinee coat trimmed with lace frills.

Ribbon: Remnant scraps of luxury-type brocade ribbon may be sewn to an envelope bag of plain silk to glamorize it for evening.

Embroidered ribbon can add charm to a plain dress for a little girl.

Diagram 130. Ribbon-trimmed dress.

Nylon Ruffle: Add rows of this to the neck and cuffs of a plain housecoat.

Diagram 131. Ruffle trim.

Ric-Rac Braid. This is available in different sizes and colours. It makes an attractive trim for children's clothes or household linens. Some effects are shown in diagram 132.

Diagram 132. (*a*) Two colours inverwoven. (*b*) Three shades wedged together. (*c*) Two lengths 'chained' together with french knot embroidery (see diagram 31). (*d*) Two wide and two narrow lengths, suitable for trimming table-cloths or curtains.

Diagram 129

Diagram 130

Diagram 131

Broderie Anglaise: This is available in various widths and patterns.

Diagram 133. (*a*) Collar and cuffs made of embroidered frilling. (*b*) Ribbon-threaded *Broderie Anglaise* trimming a little girl's dressing-gown.

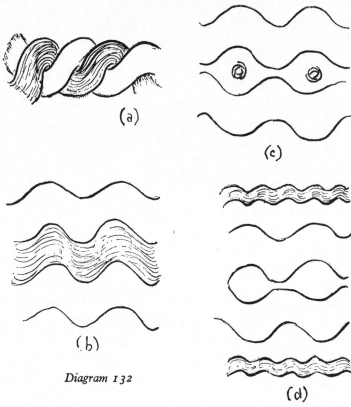

(a)

(c)

(b)

Diagram 132

(d)

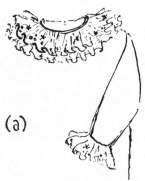

(a)

Diagram 133

Monograms: Any plain towel, scarf or handkerchief would become a prized possession if monogrammed exclusively. Transfers are available for plain or fancy lettering. If you box the letters in geometric shapes, such as triangles, squares or circles, the effect is more dramatic. Remember to work the stitching closely to withstand washing.

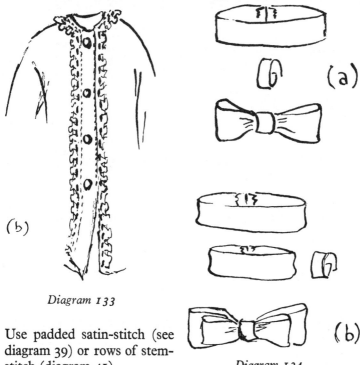

(a)

(b)

Diagram 133

Diagram 134

Use padded satin-stitch (see diagram 39) or rows of stem-stitch (diagram 41).

Wool. Strands of thick knitting wool, sewn through the centre, make an attractive collar for a plain dress. Alternatively the wool may be wound over a 3-inch card and sewn in loop form (through the double centre) to a coat for collar and cuffs.

Beads: Many splendid trimmings are available by the yard for trimming knitwear or evening clothes. Bead fringes and matching braids are also on sale and they add great luxury to garments.

Bows: These should be made in separate pieces if being used for trimming. This avoids irregularity and unnecessary thickness in the centre.

Diagram 134. (*a*) Make circle with seam inside for main section, then cover centre and seam with a separate piece, sewn

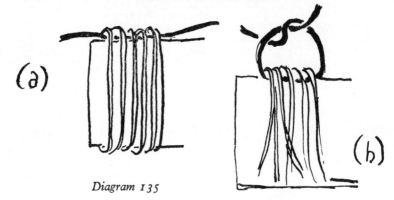

(a)

(b)

Diagram 135

at the back. (*b*) Double bow, make of two different size circles, with ends wedged between and the smaller circle centre covered before sewing together.

This type of bow is ideal for attaching to hair combs or clips.

Tassels: These are popular as trimming.

(c)

Diagram 135. (*a*) Wind wool round card. (*b*) Cut through one end. (*c*) Bind the other end securely before fastening off.

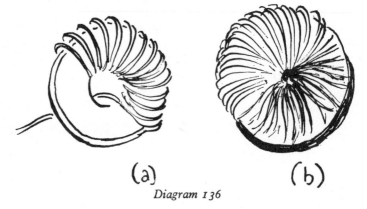

(a)   (b)

Diagram 136

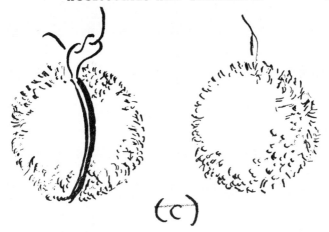

Diagram 136

Pom-Pons: Children love these on their caps and they make soft balls for baby.

Diagram 136 (*a*) Wind wool over two card circles (with one-third diameter cut from centre) until hole is filled. (*b*) Cut edge. (*c*) Tie centre and remove card circles, then trim ends.

CHAPTER 12

Renovations and Repairs

IF you can manage alterations yourself you can save time and money. Besides adjusting hem lengths in new garments you can prolong the life of old favourites by renovating them.

Some helpful hints are given here and when you understand the processes you should be able to tackle other sewing problems with confidence.

HEMS

It is most important that this is done expertly and there are no short cuts to a satisfactory result.

Shortening Length: Do not turn up the existing hem, but unpick the stitching and press out the folds. Pin up the new length and allow the same width of hem as before, then cut off the excess material. The various ways of sewing hems are given in diagrams 105 to 107, depending on the thickness of your fabric.

Lengthening Garment: Unpick the existing hem and press to check on the amount of material available for the alteration. If there is insufficient to make a reasonably wide hem, then it is best to make a false hem. Cut a bias strip the width required and long enough to go all round hem. See diagram 108 for cutting and joining bias. Face the lower edge with bias as shown in diagram 115.

Curved Hem: After turning in the required amount to wrong side it is advisable to tack inside the fold. The fullness at the inner edge should be formed into tiny pleats that so the fabric will lie flat to stitching.

Diagram 137. Curved Hem ready for Sewing. This type of

hem should not be turned under at the inner edge and the stitches should be long and loose. If the fabric is likely to fray oversew the edge.

An effective method of lengthening or widening children's dresses is shown in diagram 138.

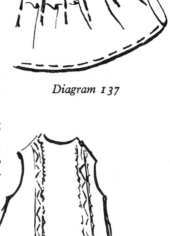

Diagram 137

Diagram 138. (*a*) Insert a band of embroidered braid in a matching colour to lengthen a dress. (*b*) To widen a bodice cut through the sides and insert lace. If the armholes are tight as well, insert the extra width in the side-seam instead.

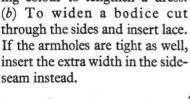

Diagram 138

Worn Edges: If the edges of a fur coat are showing signs of wear you can enclose them in matching wool braid.

If the collar and cuffs of a housecoat are soiled and worn, remove these and use the pieces to cut a facing in toning satin or velvet.

Face the pieces by turning in the edges and oversewing (see diagram 12) or working stab-stitch (see diagram 10) through both layers. Sew collar and cuffs back in position.

Sleeves can be removed from garments and the armhole faced with bias. Remember to draw up the armhole slightly with a gathering thread under the arm before facing. See diagram 115 for facing.

Necklines: If too loose, can be re-faced. Unpick the stitching, gather round neckline very slightly and stay-stitch, then re-face with smaller facing. If too tight, it is easier to adjust. Unpick the facing edge and re-sew seam $\frac{1}{4}$ inch inside the original seam. Trim away the original seam. Be careful not to make the neck too large ($\frac{1}{4}$ inch will make it $1\frac{1}{2}$ inches larger).

If the back of a zipped neckline is inclined to gape, undo the zip stitching nearly to the end, then fold back the excess fabric, tapering it off to meet the lower edge each side of the zip and re-sew.

Waistline: If too loose, take the excess into the side-seam, tapering the fullness to armhole and hem. If too tight, it may be possible to release some fabric from the side seams by sewing the seams narrower. The stitching lines (from previous seams) can generally be removed by rubbing the fabric over with a damp cloth before pressing.

Frayed Sleeve Edges: For men's wear, leather strips are available with punched holes for sewing. These are merely folded over the edge and stab-stitched (see diagram 10). For women's clothes, matching wool braid could be used, but they could also be turned in a fraction. Unpick the lining and facing and press open. Lightly darn over the worn edge on the wrong side with matching wool. Turn back inside, with the frayed edge just inside the sleeve and press fold. Re-sew in position then hem the lining over facing.

Jacket Pockets: If the edges are frayed, cover with leather as for sleeves. If the lining is worn this can be replaced; unpick the lower edge of the lining and cut off the worn section of the pocket. Use this as a pattern to cut new section, allowing 1 inch for joining and $\frac{1}{2}$ inch for remaining seams. Join new sections together then join to old pocket with a run and fell seam (see diagram 110).

Trouser Pockets: Remove the worn pocket and use as a pattern to cut new fabric – use strong fabric such as twill. Sew the straight edge of each pocket section to the garment first, then join the pieces together on the wrong side. Clip the curves and press. Torn sections can be replaced as given for jacket pockets on previous page. Alternatively new pockets can be bought to replace completely worn ones.

Children's Pockets: Line these with plastic which can be wiped clean when sticky from confectionery.

Frayed Turn-ups: Unpick the hems and press flat. If the material is reversible, press the turn-up to the right side and catch-stitch (see diagram 105). When the trouser end is turned up again and pressed, the frayed edge will come inside the fold. It may be necessary to catch the turn-up in position at each seam. Alternatively, open the hem and darn the frayed edge from the wrong side, then fold the end up inside again, but arranging the frayed section to come inside the fold. Cover the frayed section with a strip of leather – stab-stitch this in position before sewing the inside hem (see diagram 10 for stab-stitch).

Frayed Collars: Unpick the neckband to release the collar. If the collar is reversible turn it round and re-sew into the neckband. If the collar is not reversible, use the shape to cut a new section from the tail of the shirt, allowing $\frac{1}{2}$ inch all round. Place new section over collar and turn extensions over to the wrong side along outer and side edges. Mitre the corners (see diagram 7), turn under $\frac{1}{4}$ inch and hem (see diagram 8). Machine-stitch all round these sides from the right side, near the edge. Re-sew collar to neckband. Hem the shirt tail after straightening edge.

New collars are available to replace completely worn ones and these should be sewn to neckband as explained above. If required, stiff collars could be worn if the neckband is sewn along the top edge and a buttonhole made in the centre back of band for collar stud. See diagram 111 for buttonhole-stitch.

Frayed Cuffs: These can usually be repaired quite easily. Unpick the edge stitching and $\frac{1}{2}$ inch in side seams. Push the frayed edge inside the double fabric and oversew the edge (see diagram 12) then stitch through both layers inside edge as remainder of cuff. *Double Cuffs.* Reverse these as explained for collars. New cuffs are available to replace completely worn ones and these should be sewn to the sleeve edge as existing cuff.

Split Lining: When the fabric is frayed, strengthen it with ribbon or tape backing and stitch over the frayed section in a zig-zag manner, attaching the backing at the same time.

Frayed Welts: Fold the welt in half to the wrong side and catch-stitch the frayed edge to the top of the welt.

Torn Lace: Back this with net and run-stitch over the pattern, attaching the backing.

Torn Leather: Use a very fine needle and matching thread. Work buttonhole stitch all along the torn edges (see diagram 20) then oversew the purl edges of the buttonholing together.

Worn Elastic: Replacements are available for suspenders, bra fastenings and panties. Remove worn elastic and replace with new.

Darning: Small holes and threadbare sections can be adequately mended with darning. Use the same thread as the material being repaired.

Diagram 139

Diagram 139: Darning. First darn vertically, starting outside the weakened edge and working parallel to the threads in the fabric. Leave a small loop at each turn. When all the vertical darning is complete, work the horizontal rows in the same way (parallel to the fabric thread and leaving small loops at each turn) but weave the needle in and out of the vertical threads alternately as shown.

Corner Tear: Darn in and out vertically over the horizontal tear and in and out horizontally over the vertical tear, thus reinforcing the corner with double stitching.

Diagonal Tear: Darn vertically and horizontally across the tear.

Invisible Darning: This should be done with threads from the seams. Darn in each direction as shown in diagram 139, but leave short ends instead of loops at each turn, on the wrong side of fabric.

Blanket Holes: Darn these as given in diagram 139, using matching embroidery wool.

Blanket Edges: If worn, these may be turned in and wide buttonhole stitch worked over the hem (see diagram 20*a*). Alternatively the edges may be enclosed in satin binding which is available ready folded.

Shoulder Straps: If these break the end should be attached to elastic before sewing back to garment. To prevent slipping straps, sew a 2-inch long piece of narrow elastic to shoulder seam at one end, and attach a press fastener to the other end of elastic to fasten to shoulder seam. Loop this around shoulder strap and fasten.

PATCHING

Patches must be made when the rent or tear is too large for darning. Use the same material as the garment being repaired if possible – you must not use a thicker fabric. Cut a square patch a little larger than the hole and tack this to the wrong side. Turn in and hem the edges (see diagram 8) then turn to the right side. Cut the hole neatly into the square shape and snip the corners so that the edges can be turned in and hemmed all round. This is ideal for patching sheets and other linens, but for repairing woollens a top-sewn patch is more suitable.

Diagram 140: Top-sewn Patch. The hole should be trimmed to fit the patch exactly, allowing $\frac{1}{2}$-inch seams. Both edges are turned to the wrong side and the folds over sewn together (see diagram 12) with matching thread. Trim away the outer corners and mitre the inner ones (see diagram 7). This type of patch may also be back-stitched.

Sheets: If these are wearing thin in the centre cut through the centre and turn the outer edges to the centre. Join centre

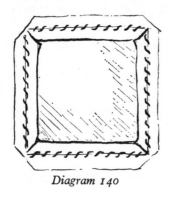

Diagram 140

with a run and fell seam (see diagram 110) and hem the outer edges (see diagram 8).

Pillow-cases. If these are weakened at the seams bind the edges with contrast cotton, mitring the corners (see diagram 7).

Replacing Zip. Remove old zip and oversew the edges of material so that they lie flat. Sew new zip behind then undo the oversewing.

Old Nylons: Use these, washed and cut up, to fill cushion pads and to stuff toys.

Leather Buttons: These are expensive to buy and can be made from an odd glove. The base is available in different sizes and instructions are included for the covering of these.

Remaking Garments: If using old garments to make children's clothes, unpick all the seams and press fabric flat before cutting new sections. Avoid any worn sections when arranging new pattern pieces.

Part 4

HOME MAKES

CHAPTER 13

Soft Furnishings

CURTAINS are the most important feature in furnishing any room, and these can echo your personality.

No complicated shaping and cutting out is involved in the making and they are easy to sew when you are aware of the correct procedure.

If you can sew the curtains yourself you can make the most of each window. Ugly shapes can be disguised and curtaining can create illusions of width and height.

Most windows need sheer drapes for screening the glass and heavy curtains to draw at night. Both types are dealt with in this chapter.

Spend time considering the type of fabric for each room. The colours should blend with the walls and floor covering and the pattern must not conflict with other furnishings. If the furniture upholstery is patterned the curtaining should be plain, unless the curtains are to be made in the same material as the upholstery.

The length and style is important too. You can have floor length curtains to add dignity to a bedroom, lounge, or dining-room or curtains just below the sill for nursery, kitchen or bathroom. Pelmets are optional nowadays because there are so many interesting headings.

Measuring for Curtains: First measure the height. For short curtains measure to 3 inches below window-sill. To the total height add 5 inches (for the hem and heading); this also allows for possible shrinkage. Now measure the width, allowing for the overlap in the centre when curtains are drawn. Allow twice the width for fine fabrics and $1\frac{1}{2}$ times the width for heavy fabrics. Additional material required to make up the width should be added equally to the outside of each curtain. The matching of patterns usually requires extra material, unless the repeat divides equally into the length of each piece. For cross-over drapes extra length must be allowed, depending on the width of the window; usually the drape requires $\frac{1}{3}$ of the total length. Check this with a piece of string, assuming that the curtains will overlap for one-third of the width in the centre. Take the string from the cross-over point and let it drape to the side where the curtain will tie.

The same amount of lining must be bought. This is available in colours or white.

Lining: This makes a world of difference to curtains. It makes the fabric drape gracefully, prevents fading and makes them last longer, also, it helps to exclude draughts. This takes time, but is well worth all the effort in the end.

First join the curtaining and lining into the correct widths and press seams. If the curtain selvedges are inclined to pull, snip these every 3 inches or so.

Place the curtain, right side down, on the floor (or a large flat non-slip surface). Turn in one side edge 1 inch and pin. Also turn in the top edge $\frac{1}{2}$ inch and tack in position. Now add the lining, right side uppermost. Turn in the top edge $\frac{1}{2}$ inch and place this edge just below the top edge of curtain. Turn in side edge 1 inch and tack the edge $\frac{1}{2}$ inch in from curtain edge. Smooth the lining over the curtain for 24 inches and pin at this point from top to bottom edge. Turn lining back and lock lining to curtain along fold as shown in diagram 141, excluding lower hem allowance.

Diagram 141. Take long buttonhole-stitches (see diagram 20) through the extreme edge of the fold and through one or two threads in the curtaining. This stitching must not show through on the right side. Leave the stitches fairly loose and make them about 1 inch apart.

Continue locking the lining to the curtaining every 24 inches throughout the width. Finally turn in the other end of curtain

Fur fabric hood *(see page 98)*

Fur fabric beret and cravat
(see page 96)

Mohair beret *(see page 6)*

Doll's dress, pampered pussy-cat, bobble birds and miniature mouse
(see page 181)

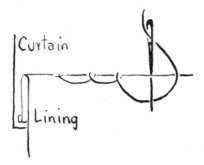

Diagram 141

and lining as previous edge. Hem the lining to the curtaining along top and side edges. Fold up hem along lower edge and hem lining over curtaining.

Certain fine fabrics, such as pure silk or satin, look much richer if they are interlined. When this is done the lining is locked to the interlining. Interlining is a type of flannelette.

Pelmets: These should be at least one-eighth of the total curtain length. They can be made absolutely straight or shaped, depending on the fabric. If the fabric is elaborately patterned, the pelmet is best left straight. However, if the curtains are to hang in four lengths in a bay window, then the pelmet could be shaped in the corners and at each other edge to correspond.

Diagram 142: Some Pelmet Shapes for Reference. Pelmets should be interlined with a special canvas – this becomes adhesive when dampened and the fabric can be ironed on to it.

Cut the pelmet canvas to the exact shape required, joining where necessary. Cut fabric to the same shape, but allow 1 inch for turnings all round. Cut lining as fabric.

Place the fabric on a flat surface, right side down, and place the canvas on top, with the turnings projecting all round. Weight the materials down. Dampen the edge of the canvas in sections and turn the fabric over on to the canvas and iron immediately. Continue in this way all around the pelmet, pleating the corners to lie flat. Turn in the lining all round and

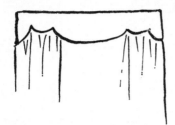

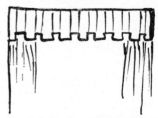

Diagram 142

slip-stitch to fabric turning near edge (see diagram 106 for slip-stitch).

Headings: Pleated or gathered headings may be used instead of pelmets. They add height to a room and can be quickly effected with the right type of tape and fittings.

Diagram 143: Gathered. This is the most economical heading as far as the amount of fabric is concerned. Sew type of Rufflette tape to wrong side, 1 inch from curtain top. This tape has two draw strings which are pulled up to gather the fabric as required. Do not cut off the draw strings, but knot these and push inside tape. Curtains can then be opened out flat for ironing, etc.

Diagram 144: Shirred. Use more than one Rufflette tape for this effect. This is best on plain fabrics.

Diagram 145: Pinch Pleated. This is most effective on heavy full-length curtains. It is quickly done with special tape and long pronged hooks. These are available in two kinds – one with a high hook for hanging curtain below

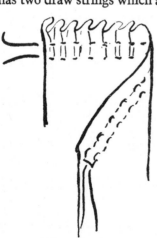

Diagram 143

the rail as in diagram, or another with a low hook which raises the curtain top above the fitment. This type of pleating reduces the width by half.

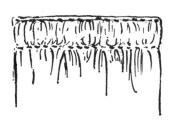

Diagram 144

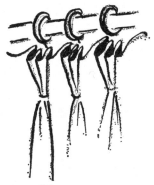

Diagram 145

Narrow Pleating. This is more suitable for short-length curtains in fine fabric. It is done with special tape and four-pronged hooks. The amount of fabric used may be varied according to the spacing of the hooks.

Diagram 146: Scalloped. This is popular for the café-type curtain, screening half the window, or for screening doors against strong sun. Use a saucer or plate to get the curve and bind the edges with matching bias (see page 3).

Diagram 147: Cross-Over Curtains. These are very elegant over large areas of glass. The centre edge must be $1\frac{1}{2}$ times the length (to allow for the drape across). To cut this type of curtain, mark the outer edge for total length required (including

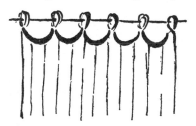

Diagram 146

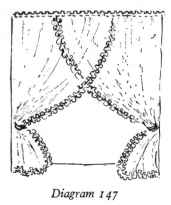

Diagram 147

heading and hem). Fold fabric from this marking to point on centre edge, then cut along the diagonal fold. To ensure an even drape overlap one-half of each curtain in the centre and make the top hem over the doubled fabric.

Diagram 148. Tucked Curtains. Ideal for obscuring an ugly view, yet not excluding the light. Calculate the double depth of each tuck required and add this to the total length.

HINTS

Trimmings can add the decorator touch to curtains. These are available in braid and fringe form, in cotton, rayon or silk, and should be matched to fabric colour.

If the curtain shrinks in cleaning, beyond the extent of the hem allowance, then add a decorative fringe to the lower edge.

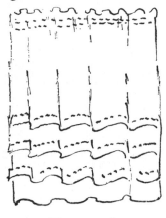

Diagram 148

Allow 1 inch per foot for shrinkage in cotton net. Terylene will not shrink and does not require starching, so is worth considering first.

Hems in net and sheer curtains should be folded double so that no edge is visible through the folds.

Weights in varying sizes are available for sewing into hems of heavy curtains to make them hang well.

Use cords for drawing curtains – these can be fixed to the curtain track and prevent handling the fabric.

A narrow strip of stiffening fabric sewn in the edge seams will keep the edge firm and straight.

Interline headings with vilene if the fabric is soft – this will enable the heading to stand upright.

Hang curtains for a few days before hemming them, to allow for any possible drop in the fabric.

Net is best sewn by hand, but if a machine is to be used, back the fabric with paper which can be torn away afterwards.

Terry-towelling makes ideal bathroom curtains and plastic is available in many suitable patterns for shower curtains.

Gingham and other washable fabrics are best for nursery curtains.

Velvet curtains should be made with the pile facing upwards to look rich and absorb the light.

BEDSPREADS

These are cheaper to make than to buy. Very little sewing is involved, and you will find a great variety of materials from which to choose, in both colour and texture.

Diagram 149: Candlewick Bedspread. This is easy to make, involving only two straight seams and a narrow hem all round.

Materials : Double Bed, 5 yards of 48-inch-wide fabric. Single Bed, 5 yards of 36-inch wide fabric. Trimming: Double size, $10\frac{1}{2}$ yards of 2-inch-wide fringe and 5 yards $\frac{1}{2}$-inch braid; Single size, 9 yards of 2-inch-wide fringe and 5 yards $\frac{1}{2}$-inch braid. Matching sewing-thread.

Making Up: Cut fabric in two lengths across the width. Fold one piece in half lengthways and cut along the fold. Join one narrow piece to each side of centre piece with a plain seam (see page 85) on right side. Cover this seam with the braid trimming, hemmed each side (see diagram 8 for hemming). Round off corners.

Turn in $\frac{3}{4}$ inch to wrong side all round, turn under $\frac{1}{4}$ inch and hem. Sew fringe over hem, joining short ends neatly.

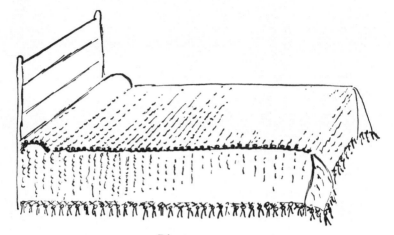

Diagram 149

Diagram 150: Quilted and Flounced Bedspread.

Materials: Double Bed, 8½ yards 48-inch-wide fabric; Single Bed, 7½ yards of 48-inch-wide fabric. Quilting: Double Bed, domette and lining, 54 by 72 inches; Single Bed, domette and lining 42 by 72 inches. Matching sewing-thread.

Cutting Out. Make up bed first. Cut fabric to fit top of bed, allowing turnings and 6 inches for tuck-in at head of bed. If

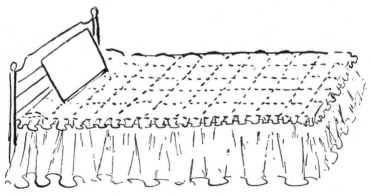

Diagram 150

fabric is not wide enough to cut the panel in one piece add extra width calculating the seam to come where the 6-inch pattern will be quilted. Measure height for flounce, allowing 2 inches for seam and hem. Cut flounce $1\frac{1}{2}$ times the width on three sides of the bed, to allow for the fullness. Cut frill 6 inches wide and the same length as flounce.

Quilting: Rule (or fold and press) top section into 6-inch squares throughout. Quilt the three layers, top, interlining and lining, together as shown on page 52.

Making Up: Frill. Join pieces into one long strip with plain seams on the wrong side. See page 85 for plain seam. Press seams open. Fold strip, wrong side inside and press fold. Gather raw edges together and draw up to fit three sides of centre piece. Tack frill to right side of centre, raw edges together.

Flounce: Join pieces as for frill. Gather top edge to fit and pin over the frill, right side inside. Sew the three layers together firmly $\frac{1}{2}$ inch from edge. Remove pins and tacking thread.

Try bedspread over made-up bed to check hem measurement for flounce. Turn in and hem edges then press hems. See diagram 106 for slip-stitch hem. Face the remaining edge (top of bed) of flounce and centre with a bias strip as shown in diagram 115. Cover raw edges of seam with a flat strip of bias, folded and hemmed each side.

Diagram 151: Dressing-Table Skirt. This is a useful disguise for a home-made dressing-table. It can be attached to a plain shelf or to the curtain rails already fitted to some whitewood furniture.

Fabric for this should be crisp so that it will flute prettily. Also, it should be washable. Two layers may be used, such as gingham covered with organza, for a very full effect.

Materials. Measure the depth from table to floor, add 3 inches for hem and seam. Measure round the table-top and double this for the width required. Fabric should be cut across the width and seamed to make up the length – it will fall better this way. The skirt should be made in two pieces, with an

Diagram 151

opening at the centre front so that the drawers or space underneath is accessible.

Measure the table-top or make a pattern of this from newspaper. Allow $\frac{1}{2}$ inch all round for seam. Cut out the fabric with
this pattern.

Gather the skirt-top and join to table-top with a plain seam
(see page 85). Press seam. Place over table to check measurement for hem. Turn in and hem required amount, also hem
back edge of top (see diagram 106 for slip-stitch hem). The
hem should be wide to make the fabric hang well.

Cover the top with plate glass to keep it clean.

If the dressing-table has a curtain rail, make up the skirt as
given for gathered curtains (diagram 143).

An alternative method is to fix the skirt to the board of the
table top with popper tape (sewn to curtain top and nailed to
board). This should then be covered with a pelmet-type top
for a neat finish.

The dressing-table skirt should be lined if the fabric chosen is soft. Lining is shown in diagram 141.

CUSHIONS

These add comfort in the home and are especially favoured for modern décor. Plastic cushions are useful for the beach too.

Attractive cushions can be made from small remnants or from pieces of discarded evening dresses. All fabrics are suitable, but delicate silks should be restricted to decorative bedroom cushions.

Cushions are expensive to buy, yet they are quick and easy to sew, and make ideal gifts for home- or garden-lovers.

Cushion Pad. This is very important. Unless it is adequately made and filled it does not serve its purpose well.

Materials: Unbleached calico or down-proof cambric. If old fabric is to be utilized work over the wrong side with household soap before stitching.

Size: Make the pad 1 inch larger than the cushion cover – this ensures that it fills out the shape adequately.

Fillings: Feathers (from old quilts or pillows), down, foam rubber clippings or kapok. The latter is the cheapest type of filling and is extremely serviceable if you disperse all the lumps (by pulling them apart) before you use it for filling.

Making Up: This should follow the pattern for the cushion it is to fill, excluding any piping or trimming. It must be packed tightly with the filling, especially in the corners, before sewing up the opening.

UNTRIMMED SQUARE CUSHION

Cut two squares of the required size. Place these together, right sides inside, and join together with a plain seam (see page 85) ½ inch from the edge, leaving an opening one side.

Turn out to the right side and press seams. Insert pad and oversew (see diagram 12) the opening neatly.

Piping Cord. This adds a professional finish to cushions and chair covers. It saves wear and tear from friction.

Before covering the cotton cord (which is available in several thicknesses) this should be boiled then dried out. This shrinks the cord and prevents it puckering the fabric afterwards.

Cover the cord with bias strips (see diagram 108 for cutting and joining bias), and tack the bias close up to the cord. Allow sufficient bias to be enclosed in the seam, say $\frac{1}{2}$ inch beyond tacking.

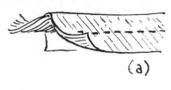

(a)

Diagram 152. (a) Piping cord covered with bias. (b) Piping being inserted in seam.

Inserting Piping. Pin the covered piping between the two pieces of material, with the right sides inside and the raw edges level (see diagram 152b). Sew through all the layers with stab-stitch (see diagram 10) or use a piping foot on the machine, keeping the stitching as close to the cord as possible. If being inserted round a curve or corner, clip the bias covering to enable the cord to lie quite flat. To join the ends of piping

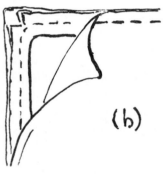

(b)

Diagram 152

cord, sew the bias together on the wrong side then trim the cord to lie level inside the seam.

PIPED CUSHION (see photograph between pages 86 and 87).

This cushion is made of velvet with piping covered in the same fabric.

Cut two squares of the required size, then cover sufficient cord with a bias strip of velvet, to go all round the square.

Place the squares together, right sides inside, inserting the piping cord as described above, and leaving an opening one side.

Turn out to the right side and steam out any creases made in the working. Insert pad then slip-stitch opening behind the piping (see diagram 106 for slip-stitch).

CIRCULAR CUSHION

This shape is best made with a gusset all round, otherwise the edges are inclined to pucker.

Diagram 153: Circular cushion trimmed with ruching.

Materials: Two circles of fabric, each 16 inches in diameter and a strip 3 by 48 inches for gusset. 2¾ yards of ruching. Matching thread.

Diagram 153

Cutting Circles: Make a pattern of newspaper. Fold a 16-inch square into four. Use a ruler to mark 8 inches from apex along each fold and at intervals across the section. Connect the markings and cut out circle. This may also be done with a compass if available.

Making Up: Pin ruching to right side of one circle and tack in position all round (see diagram 64 for tacking-stitch). Now join gusset to circle along one edge as described in diagram 126, stab-stitching through the three layers together ½ inch from edge (see diagram 10 for stab-stitch). Join short ends of gusset with a plain seam (see page 85).

Tack ruching to right side of remaining circle, then join circle to edge of gusset as before, leaving an opening for pad. Turn out to right side and insert cushion pad, made as cushion but without ruching (see page 127) then slip-stitch opening behind the ruching (see diagram 106 for slip-stitch).

These shapes may be varied considerably as required. Stripes and checks add gaiety in a group of plain cushions, and many exciting trimmings may be added to the basic shapes.

Instead of slip-stitching covers after inserting pads, the

openings may be fastened with burr tape, light-weight zip fasteners or press studs. These fastenings are suggested for covers that have to be laundered frequently. Remember that silk fringe should be dry cleaned and always test braids to see if they are colour-fast before washing covers.

CHAPTER 14

Upholstery

KNOWING how to cope with this type of sewing will give you tremendous satisfaction, because you will be able to brighten up old furniture with the minimum expenditure.

Begin with a simple item so that you will not get discouraged, and when you see how easy it is to upholster you will be able to tackle the more advanced type of thing.

Choose firmly woven fabric for upholstery to resist wear and dust. Plain fabrics are most economical and small all-over patterns are easier to handle.

DINING-CHAIR SEAT COVER

Diagram 154: Drop-in Type Chair-seat. This is the easiest job to tackle if you are a beginner, and it can give new life to an old chair.

Remove the drop-in seat and carefully undo the covering. This may be sewn or nailed in position, but is generally easy enough to remove.

Use the removed cover as a pattern to cut the new fabric. If the seat padding needs renewing as well, do this with sheets of plastic foam.

Lay the fabric on a flat

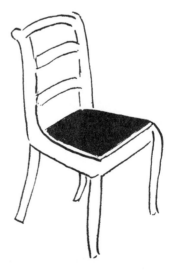

Diagram 154

surface, right side down, and place the chair seat in the centre (wrong side uppermost). Fold the fabric over the seat on all sides, mitring the corners (see diagram 7), and fasten the turnings to the frame with small tintacks. Cover the wrong side with a piece of strong fabric, turning in the edge all round and slip-stitching to cover, near the edge. Use a long thin needle for the sewing and see diagram 106 for slip-stitch.

STOOL COVER

Diagram 155: Tartan Cover with Self Fringe. The pattern is given for a round stool, 12 inches in diameter, but it can be adapted to any size required.

Materials: Use tartan wool cloth which fringes well. You will need a circle, 13 inches in diameter (see page 129 for cutting circle shape), and two strips 3 by 40 inches; matching sewing-thread and 20 upholstery studs. If the stool is not padded you will also need some foam rubber sheeting for this.

Making Up: Place the strips together and machine-stitch (or backstitch as shown in diagram 3) these together through the centre. Pin the doubled edge to the circle (right sides inside) and join with a plain seam $\frac{1}{2}$ inch from edge (see diagram 126 for joining straight edge to curve). Join short ends together. Press seams.

Diagram 155

Turn out to right side and draw away the threads from lower edge (from both layers) up to stay-stitching, for fringe.

Place cover over stool, padding inside if necessary, then attach to stool frame with upholstery pins placed 2 inches apart above fringe.

If required piping cord may be inserted in the seam.

TIE-ON CUSHION SEATS

Diagram 156. This type of cushion is very popular for windsor chairs. If you are able to make the cushion yourself, you can save money when buying the chair.

Materials: A cretonne is ideal and the padding can be layers of foam rubber sheeting.

Make a paper pattern of the seat shape and use this to cut out the fabric, allowing $\frac{1}{2}$ inch all round for seam. Cut two pieces alike and a straight strip, about 2 inches wide, to go all round the shape. Cut four pieces, each 3 by 10 inches for ties and sufficient bias to cover piping cord to go round the shape twice.

Making Up: Make up cushion as given for round cushion on page 129, but insert piping cord instead of ruching in each seam. Cut foam rubber to shape and

Diagram 156

Diagram 157

use more than one layer to make up the depth. Insert this then close opening.

Ties: Fold each in half lengthways, right sides inside, and join long side $\frac{1}{2}$ inch from edge. Turn out to right side. Turn in ends and oversew (see diagram 12). Sew ties to corners of cushion to tie in a bow around chair struts.

TAILORED CUSHIONS

Diagram 157. These are simple shapes to re-make when the covering is worn. Remove the old cover and use to cut new fabric. Make up as described for piped cushion and cushion with gusset on pages 128, 129.

COVERED BEDHEAD

Diagram 158

Diagram 158. This gives a luxury-look to a plain bed. It can be made to cover any shape. Glazed chintz, or fabric with a silicone finish is most suitable.

Materials: Make a paper pattern of the bedhead to be covered to assess the quantity of fabric required. You will need two pieces 1 inch larger than measurement of bed-head. In addition you will need a straight strip long enough to go all round three sides and wide enough to cover width of bed-head, plus 1 inch for seams. Extra fabric for bias strips to cover piping cord to go in seams, to bind lower edges and cover buttons. For the lining, cotton wadding the same size as bed-head and muslin lining. For the buttoning you may cover small moulds, or use flat pearl buttons with shanks. Matching sewing-thread.

Making Up: Place one main section, right side up, on a flat surface and mark positions for buttons. These should be in alternate rows, 6 inches apart. Now join three layers thus: place fabric right side down, cover with wadding and muslin. Tack the three layers together all round (see diagram 64 for tacking-stitch). Turn to right side and sew buttons over markings, indenting the fabric.

Make up the front and back sections with gusset and piping

as given for round cushion on page 129. Bind the lower edges. Attach narrow ties to front and back each side to tie under headboard.

This is a big job to undertake, but it is not difficult if you tackle it step-by-step. The results will be invaluable in preserving good furniture or covering worn pieces.

Materials: The fabric should be washable and it is usual to use 48-inch-wide fabric. Cretonne is always popular for covers, but repp or linen would be equally suitable. Large patterns are extravagant because the motif has to be centralized throughout. Plain fabrics are easiest to plan if you are inexperienced.

The average easy chair takes about 6 yards of 48-inch fabric, this includes allowance for bias covering of piping cord. Carefully measure each section of the chair and write down the measurement, adding 2 inches for seams and 6 inches for tuck-in around seat.

It is simplest to build the pattern over the actual chair and cut off each section as it is fitted adequately. Follow the diagram and key step-by-step. Keep the selvedge of the fabric at the side throughout and ensure that the grain is straight on each section. If a patterned fabric is being used, centralize motifs on the back, seat and inside each arm. Mark centre of back and seat with chalk line.

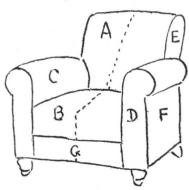

Diagram 159: Loose Cover Plan. (*a*) Double fabric. Place fold to centre back, smooth fabric over top to back seam and down to seat. Allow for seams and tuck-in, then cut away

Diagram 159

excess. (*b*) Double fabric. Place fold to centre and smooth fabric to back and front edge. Allow for seams and tuck-in, then cut away excess. (*c*) Single fabric. Smooth fabric over top to seam on outside edge, then down to seat. Allow for seams and tuck-in, then cut away excess. Make both arm sections in the same way, remembering to 'face' the pattern. (*d*) Single fabric. Pin to shape, taking the lower edge down to bottom of chair. Allow turnings then cut away excess. Make the opposite section in the same way, matching the pattern. (*e*) Cut the sides of back in the same way as (*d*). (*f*) Single fabric. Place top to seam outside arm, allowing 2 inches for seam. Smooth fabric to side and lower edges. Allow turnings and cut away excess. Cut the other side the same way. (*g*) Double fabric. Place fold to centre of front section, smooth fabric to all three sides. Allow turnings then cut away excess.

Back of Chair. Double fabric. Place fold to centre, beginning at top seam, and smooth to side and lower edge. Allow for turnings then cut away excess.

Making Up. Pin all sections together on wrong side, leaving one back seam open. Make tiny pleats in the straight edges being attached to (*d*) and (*e*), and snip the edges to make them lie flat.

Place pinned cover over chair, right side inside. Pin the back opening. Adjust the pins until the cover fits exactly over the seams. Push the tuck-in sections well into the crevices. Ask someone to sit in the chair to check if there is any strain on any seam. Release fabric if this is the case. Do not remove the cover from the chair until a perfect fit is obtained everywhere.

Unpin the back side seam sufficiently to be able to remove the cover from the chair. Trim all seams to 1 inch.

At this stage measure the amount of piping cord required. This should be prepared as shown in diagram 152. Each seam piped on the chair should be piped on the cover. Piping adds a professional finish and resists wear and tear.

To insert the piping cord unpin the relevant seams in small sections and pin the piping cord in position. See diagram 152.

Join all seams, excepting back opening. Sew popper tape to this opening, or a zip fastener may be used instead.

The lower edge may be finished with piping or trimmed with matching fringe.

Alternatively, gathered or pleated frill may be added. Measure the depth and add allowance for hem and seam. Measure all round chair and double the measurement for pleating ($1\frac{1}{2}$ times for gathered frill).

Settee: The same principles apply as for Chair, but add more width and remember to match the pattern when placing panels side by side.

CHAPTER 15

Lampshade Making

THESE are surprisingly easy to make. The same principles apply whether you are making a new shade or re-covering an existing frame.

A variety of shapes, types and sizes are obtainable to suit individual requirements. When you know how to make lampshades you can happily buy suitable remnants of fabric to co-ordinate with other furnishings. You can also choose from a wide range of matching or contrasting trimmings.

Materials: No special tools are required. Satin and silk fabrics are ideal for curved lampshades because they have the right amount of stretch. Cottons and linens are best for the straight type such as drums or cylinders.

Quantities: With a few exceptions, fabric is applied to the frame on the bias, in two halves. To estimate the quantity required use newspaper. Take a sheet equal to a proportion of yardage – say 18 by 36 ($\frac{1}{2}$) or 13$\frac{1}{2}$ by 36 ($\frac{3}{8}$). Fold newspaper diagonally (see diagram 108) and cut along fold. Place this triangle over half of the frame, and you will see immediately how much fabric and lining will be needed.

Trimmings: These are used primarily to conceal the seam turnings, but also enhance the finished shade. Gimp (the straight-edge braid) is usually sewn along the top edge and fringing along the lower edge. Other popular trimmings are nylon ruffle, bobble braid, lace or flat braid.

Binding: Tape is available in natural for binding the frame. If the shade is not to be lined, use bias binding to match the colour of the cover for binding. You will need double the amount of wire to be covered for the binding. It is necessary to bind the wire frame so that the lining and cover can be sewn to the binding; it also prevents rust marks on the fabric if the shade is allowed to get damp.

Bind all the upright struts first. Begin at a junction of the wire by folding the tape around this to secure it. Wrap tape round and round, enclosing the end, and overlapping the edges slightly. Keep tape binding firm throughout. At end of strut pin the tape over the edge of frame temporarily. Bind top and lower edges, enclosing the pinned ends and removing pins.

Lining : Cut fabric diagonally (see diagram 108). Place the triangle shape over the bound frame. First pin all along top edge. Next pin one side edge. Stretch fabric well and pin lower edge. Finally pin other side.

Diagram 160 : Bias Fabric pinned to Frame. Fabric must not sag at any point. Continue stretching the fabric and adjusting the pins until the fabric is very taut throughout. Make sure that the seams will lie over the side struts.

Cut off the surplus fabric up to $\frac{1}{4}$ inch all round. Remove the

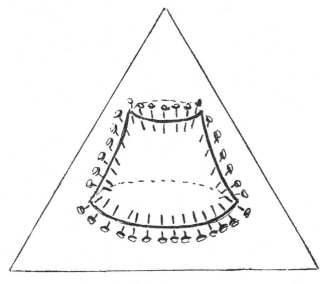

Diagram 160

lining and use this piece to cut lining for the other half of frame.

Join the side seams on the wrong side with a plain seam (see page 85) ¼ inch from the edge. Press seams.

Place lining inside the bound frame, right side inside and seams over struts. Cut a small slit each side of lining for gimbal struts. Pin lining again, making any slight adjustments. Oversew the lining to the tape as shown in diagram, using matching thread.

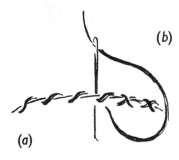

(b)

(a)

Diagram 161

Diagram 161. Hold edge of lining over bound frame and make short upright stitches from left to right through the lining and binding (*a*). Work a return row of stitching as shown in (*b*).

Cut a short bias strip of lining, fold in half lengthways and use this to cover the slit in lining at the junction of the gimbal.

Diagram 162. Sew one end over edge of lining, take strip under gimbal and sew over other edge.

Cover. Make this as described for lining. Place over lined frame, turn in edges and pin all round. Make any adjustments now. Hem (see diagram 106) all round over the lining, sewing through the lining and binding-tape.

Diagram 162

Renewing Lampshade: If this is required in the existing style, carefully remove the covering and use the pieces as a pattern to cut out the new fabric. Renew the tape on the frame if it is at all loose or worn.

BRACKET LIGHT SHADE (see photograph between pages
86 and 87)

This is an easy shape to tackle for a first attempt. The size
of the frame illustrated is 5 inches deep and 6 inches in
diameter.

Materials: ⅜ yard each of silk and lining; ⅜ yard of narrow
gimp and ⅝ yard 1-inch wide fringe; 3½ yards binding-tape
and matching thread. These materials are sufficient for one
shade only.

Making Up: Follow directions given on pages 138–40 for
binding frame, lining and cover.

Finishing: Sew gimp to top edge and fringe to lower edge,
joining seams neatly.

OVAL SHADE (see hanging lampshade in photograph
between pages 86 and 87).

The frame illustrated is 7 inches deep and 10 inches in
diameter. It is trimmed with the same contrast braid on both
edges.

Materials: ½ yard of fine satin (used for both lining and
cover); 48 inches of ¾-inch-wide velvet braid; 5 yards binding-
tape and matching sewing-thread.

Making Up: Follow directions given on pages 138–40 for
binding frame, lining and cover.

Finishing: Sew braid to top and lower edge, joining seams
neatly.

Note. If this type of shade is to be used for a table lamp, it is
not necessary to line the frame and more light will filter
through. In this instance only half the fabric will be needed for
cover.

FLUTED SHADE (see table lamp in photograph between
pages 86 and 87).

This elegant shape is covered with chiffon and trimmed with
guipure lace flowers. The frame is 9 inches deep and 12 inches
in diameter at the lower edge.

Materials : A strip of chiffon 11 by 40 inches (seams can be placed over wire struts); ⅝ yard white satin lining; 1¾ yards ¾-inch-wide white guipure lace and ½ yard ⅜-inch-wide guipure lace; 7 yards of binding-tape and matching sewing-thread.

Making Up : Follow directions given on page 139 for binding frame, and for making up the lining pieces.

Pin the lining over the bound frame, right side inside. Sew lining in position as given on page 140.

Pin the chiffon to lower edge as shown in diagram below, arranging the ends to lie over an upright strut.

Diagram 163: Fabric Pinned to Fluted Edge. Draw fabric up to the top edge and gather the edge of fabric to fit the frame. Tie around the inner edge of top cuff, then pin the fabric to top edge of frame, keeping the grain straight throughout.

Diagram 163

Trim edges to within ½ inch of frame edge. Remove cover and join side seam on wrong side.

Replace cover, turn in edges and sew to frame. Sew wide guipure lace to top and lower edge and narrow lace to inner edge of rim.

GLOBE SHADE

Diagram 164. This shade is covered with fabric to match the curtains.

For this type of cover it is not necessary to bind the frame and a painted wire frame

Diagram 164

could be used. The fabric is sewn in a straight strip and elasticated each end.

Materials : A bias strip long enough to fit around the widest part of the frame and wide enough to cover the depth. Add $\frac{1}{2}$ inch for side seam and $1\frac{1}{2}$ inches along each edge (for hems). Roll elastic.

Making Up. Join short ends of strip with a plain seam (see page 85) and press seam. Fold in $1\frac{1}{2}$ inches along each long edge, turn under $\frac{1}{2}$ inch, and hem, leaving a small opening for elastic (see diagram 106 for slip-stitch hem).

Thread elastic through hems and draw up to fit frame rings at upper and lower edge, knot elastic and tuck ends inside hems. In this way it is easily removed for laundering the lampshade cover.

CHAPTER 16

Rugmaking

THIS is an ever-popular fireside hobby for the long winter evenings. Time is needed for the making, but each member of the family can partake in the hobby.

Rugs can be made in several different ways, to make every home more cosy. A few of the interesting methods are illustrated for you to take your choice.

The life of any rug depends on the materials used, so it is worth while to use the strongest canvas and the best quality wools.

Canvas: This is available in widths from 12 to 48 inches with eight holes to one check. These widths may be joined together quite easily if required for specific measurements. Single thread canvas is also available for raffia and embroidered rugs – this has 10 holes to one inch.

Wools: These are available in cut packs (for pile rugs) or by the skein (for embroidered rugs and fringes). Approximately 6 lbs of rug wool is required to work one square yard. Two ounces will work about six square inches. Short pile, worked over a wooden gauge, is more economical and will take approximately one-quarter less than luxury pile. Woollen thrums, left over from carpet making, can also be used to make up the thickness required. The wide range of colours available in rug wool ensures the blending in of rugs with contemporary or traditional furnishings. A practical scheme (for homes where children abound) is to use light and dark wool alternately or to use the twin and triple-toned wools. Plain colours look well and for an all-over plain rug choose the same dye lot, otherwise the effect may be spoiled by a shade variation.

Tools: A latch hook for pile rugs; a rug needle for embroidery stitches; a grooved wooden gauge or circular cutter; a wooden gauge for short pile.

Designs : Illustrated catalogues of stencilled designs are obtainable at needlework departments. Alternative colours may be chosen for these designs.

TECHNIQUES

Diagram 165 : (*a*) *Knotted Pile.* This is worked with a latch hook and 2¾-inch-long strands. Loop strand evenly round shaft of hook and insert hook under the double weft threads. Slip ends of strand round the latch and across under the hook. Draw ends through the first loop and pull ends to tighten the knot. Each knot must lie in the same direction throughout the work.

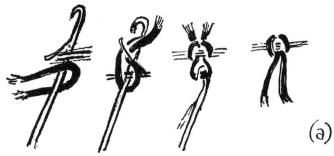

(a)

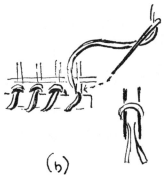

(*b*)

Diagram 165

(*b*) *Short Pile.* This is worked with a continuous strand over a narrow wooden gauge. Thread rug needle with about 1 yard length. Take needle up and down through double warp thread to form first knot. Place gauge in position below the knot. Continue making successive knots, winding the wool under the gauge each time as shown.

Move the gauge along the row as work proceeds. When row is completed remove the gauge and cut through all the loops.

(c) *Looped Pile.* This is a good way to use up oddments. Use hessian for the base and a long pencil for the loops. Thread rug needle with about 1 yard length and stitch over the pencil and through the hessian, keeping the stitches close together. Move pencil along as work proceeds. These loops are not cut, but an adhesive backing should be used to keep them securely locked on the wrong side.

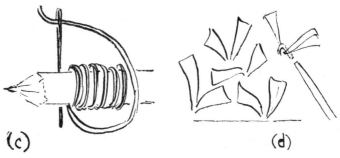

Diagram 165

(d) *Rag Rug.* This is always in style for a cottage home. Use strips of fabric, about 2 inches wide and 3 inches long. With a crochet hook draw one end through a hessian base. Continue this way until the background is completely filled, then use an adhesive backing to keep the strips firmly in place.

(e) *Nylon Rug.* A useful rug for the bathroom and a good way to use up all those laddered stockings. Cut stocking crossways into 1-inch rings, discarding the feet. Loop the rings together to form long strips. Plait three of these looped strips to-

gether and begin coiling the plait and sewing it into a flat circle. As work proceeds add more rings and plait further, until the size of rug required is obtained, then sew end to wrong side.

(*f*) *Braided Mat.* This is quickly made from 1 pound of rug wool. One skein (2 ounces) makes an effective draught excluder. Use shades of one colour or entirely one colour. Divide one hank into twenty-seven 36-inch lengths. Tie ends together securely 3 inches from one end. Braid the strands together (nine strands in each section), making a 1½-inch-wide plait. Tie 3 inches from other end. Make seven more plaits in the same way and then sew them edge to edge.

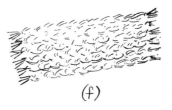

(f)

If the mat is to be used on a polished surface back it with non-skid canvas, but otherwise it is reversible.

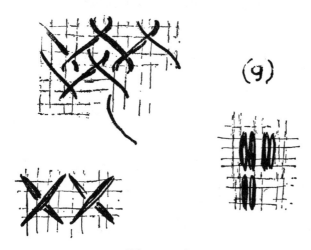

(g)

Diagram 165

(*g*) *Embroidered Rugs.* These are worked with continuous lengths over counted threads. Many stitches are suitable, particularly cross-stitch (over intersections), satin-stitch (two stitches in each hole) and herringbone-stitch (over warp threads). Tramméd canvases are also available for tapestry rugs.

Working: Canvas should be placed on a flat surface and

evenly weighted to resist the pull when making the knots. The main canvas should be away from the worker and as the rug is worked it should be turned under.

Work from left to right, completing each row right across and keeping all the stitches in the one direction throughout. At the beginning and end of pile rugs turn the raw edge of the canvas over to the right side for about 2 inches and work through both the layers to secure the fold. For embroidered rugs turn edges to the wrong side and work through the double thickness. This is not possible on curved edges, which must be faced with braid. Keep the selvedge edges each side when working and leave the folded edge free for fringing if this is required.

Joining Widths: Use a waxed thread and stab-stitch (see diagram 10) the two edges together just inside the selvedge edge.

Finishing: Selvedges and other edges (if not fringed) should be overcast with a binding-stitch.

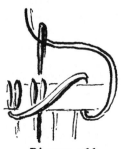

Diagram 166: Binding-Stitch. Work from left to right on wrong side. Thread rug needle with a 1-yard-length of wool. Bring needle out through the end hole. Take needle over the edge and up through the fourth hole on right. Take needle back over edge and up through the second hole. Now work through the fifth hole and back through the third. Continue in this way throughout edge.

Diagram 166

Shaped edges should be faced with binding-tape. First trim the raw edges. Use waxed thread to sew the braid over the raw edges. The inner edge will have to be pleated at intervals to make it lie flat.

Non-skid backing is available and should be used if the rugs are for polished surfaces.

Trim off any uneven tufts then wipe finished pile over with a damp cloth on right side to remove any excess fluff.

Diagram 167: Fringing. Use 8-inch-lengths of wool and a crochet hook to knot ends through loop as shown.

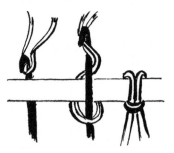

Diagram 167

CONTEMPORARY RUG
(see photograph between pages 54 and 55).

This abstract design is worked in blue, green and black from the chart given on next page. It would also look exciting worked in orange, red and brown.

Materials: Paton's Turkey Rug Wool in cut packs – 16 units black, 17 dark blue, 9 each of light blue and green. ¼ pound black Turkey Rug Wool in skeins (for fringe); 1¾ yards 27-inch wide Turkey brown check canvas; latch hook.

Measurements: 27 by 54 inches (excluding fringe). See general instructions for rugmaking on page 145 and diagram 165 for knot-stitch. Follow the chart given on next page for the pattern and colour key. Work one knot over weft threads for each symbol in the chart.

Fringe: Cut black wool into 8-inch lengths and knot through ends as shown in diagram 167. Trim fringe ends.

Diagram 168: Rug Chart.

MOSAIC RUG

Use the outlined squares on the canvas for the pattern and make a gay mosaic of jewel shades. Fill each square with a different shade and use the same quality wool throughout so that the thickness does not vary and spoil the effect.

OVAL RUG

Diagram 169. This is embroidered in double cross-stitch, forming a trellis-work of flowers.

Materials: Turkey Rug Wool in skeins: 34 ounces main

■ black ☐ dark blue

Diagram 168

$\boxed{\text{X}}$ green $\boxed{\cdot}$ light blue

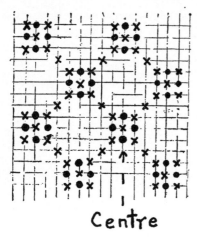

Centre

X mid contrast

● dark contrast

Diagram 169

colour, 12 ounces mid contrast (for trellis) and 6 ounces dark contrast (for flowers); 1¾ yards 27-inch wide Turkey Check Canvas: rug needle.

Measurements: 27 by 54 inches (excluding fringe).

Diagram 170: Semi-Circle. Take a square of newspaper, measuring 27 inches (or half the alternative length required). Tie a pencil to fine string and attach the end of the string to one corner of the newspaper with a pin, making sure that the pencil-point reaches to the opposite corner. Now draw a pencil line across the width up to the top left-hand corner. Cut out the quarter-circle shape.

Fold canvas in half across width and place straight edge of paper pattern to the fold. Use a coloured crayon (or contrast thread) to mark all round the curve. Reverse the canvas and mark the other side. At least two inches should be allowed outside the marking to allow for seams.

Diagram 171: Double Cross-Stitch. First work a single cross-stitch diagonally over four crossings of canvas threads, then work a second cross-stitch at right angles as shown. See general directions for rugmak-

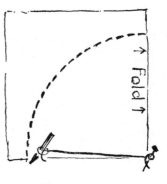

Diagram 170

Diagram 171

ing on page 144 and diagram 171 for the embroidery stitch.

Embroidery: Fold canvas across width and length to establish the centre. Thread needle with 1 yard-length of dark contrast and begin with the flower in the centre. Follow chart, diagram 169, working each double cross-stitch over a double crossing of canvas threads in each direction. Work the flower and trellis pattern first, then fill in the background.

Finishing: Trim excess canvas to within 1½ inches of edge. Turn in excess to wrong side and face with binding as shown on page 148. Work binding-stitch (see diagram 166) over selvedge edge. Trim curved edge with fringe (8-inch lengths) as shown in diagram 167.

STAIRCARPET

Diagram 172: Hungarian Stitch. Work two satin-stitches over one pair of weft threads, then work two satin-stitches over three pairs of weft threads (one more each side of first pair). Continue stitching in this way across from selvedge to selvedge. In the next row alternate the stitches as shown.

A hard-wearing staircarpet can be made from oddments of rug wool. To approximate the amount of wool required, consider that 24 ounces will be sufficient to cover 1 yard of 18-inch wide rug canvas.

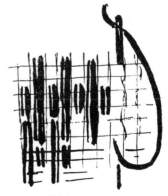

Bind the selvedges as shown in diagram 166. See general directions for rugmaking and backing on page 144.

Diagram 172

HEXAGON RUG

Diagram 173. This is made up of crocheted sections in a galaxy of colours.

Materials: 2 ounces of rug wool will make one hexagon. A No. 3 crochet hook.

Measurement: Each hexagon approximately 6 inches. Refer to crochet section on page 173 for an explanation of the abbreviations and stitch.

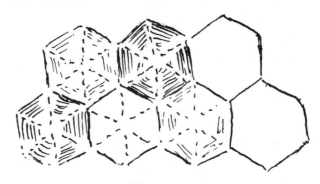

Diagram 173

Hexagon: Make 6 ch. and join into a circle with a s.s. *1st round.* (2 d.c. in each ch.) to end. Mark end of rounds with a contrast thread. *2nd round.* (1 d.c. in next st., 3 d.c. in next st.) to end. *3rd round.* (1 d.c. in each of next 2 sts., 3 d.c. in next st., 1 d.c. in next st.) to end. Continue in this way until there are 7 d.c. between each increase (60 sts.). Fasten off.

Make the number of hexagons required then join them together along one straight edge with a neutral d.c. or oversew them together on the wrong side. Press well with a warm iron over a damp cloth.

This pattern could be continued until the hexagon is large enough to make a fan-shaped cushion (folded) or a full-size hexagon one from two pieces alike.

Part 5

KNITTING AND CROCHET

CHAPTER 17

Knitting

THIS is a very practical hobby and one that can be picked up in odd moments anywhere.

Step-by-step instructions are given for absolute beginners and valuable hints are included for the experienced knitter.

Basic patterns are given, from the very first size up to 42-inch chest or bust measurement. Once the principle of knitting is clearly understood it should be possible to follow any of the standard patterns available.

Materials: Always use the materials specified in the pattern. This is very important as each pattern is written for a particular wool or yarn, which may have characteristics not suited to certain stitches and styles. Interchanging materials, without considering these facts, may have disastrous results.

TENSION

Diagram 174. This must be correct as stated in the pattern, otherwise the garment will not turn out to be the right size. Work a small square of the pattern, using the right needles and wool. Place this flat and measure the stitches with a

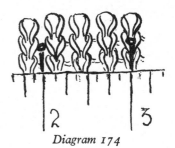

Diagram 174

ruler and pins as shown in diagram. To measure the number of rows turn to the wrong side as the purl stitches are easier to count.

If you have too many stitches to the inch, change to a larger needle and try a new sample. If there are too few stitches, try a smaller needle. Do not attempt the pattern until you have the right tension.

Make sure the needles are long enough to hold the number of stitches needed for the pattern. Needles come in various sizes.

Do not join on new wool in the middle of a row but knot this at the beginning and darn in the ends afterwards.

It is easier to count the stitches if the needles are of a different colour to the working wool or yarn.

Always measure knitting on a flat surface, and along the straight of the fabric.

Diagram 175

Diagram 175. Dropped stitches can be picked up with a crochet-hook so keep one handy.

Picking up stitches (for a neckband, etc.) needs to be done very carefully to avoid holes. Use a smaller size needle for the actual picking-up row and remember to change it to continue the pattern. Insert the point of the needle one stitch in from the edge, wind the wool round the needle and draw the stitch through on to the needle. This should be done from the right side of the work. If stitches have to be picked up from a straight cast-off edge, insert the needle through the double loops of each cast-off stitch.

When working Fair Isle patterns do not weave the wools on the wrong side – this makes the stitch uneven and is inclined to show through to the right side. Instead, carry the wool not in use along the back of work and before changing colours spread the worked stitches on the right-hand needle – this will prevent the carried wool from being too tight and puckering the work.

Inserting Zip Fasteners: The knitted fabric should cover the teeth completely. To ensure that this is so, lightly oversew the knitted edges together edge-to-edge. See that the knitted fabric is quite flat and check this on a flat surface. Place the zip fastener on the wrong side, centralizing the teeth over the seam. Sew the zip tape each side and press seam. Remove oversewing from knitted edge.

Diagram 176: Picking Up Stitches. Use a smaller needle to pick up rows of stitches, inserting the needle from the front to the back of each stitch, from the left. The stitches will then lie untwisted on the needle, in the right position for continuing the work.

Altering Knitteds: To renew a welt or cuff, unpick the seams to allow the work to lie flat. Pull out a thread right across the work immediately above the ribbing. Pick up the stitches (see diagram 176) of the upper section and work the new ribbing downwards. Cast off loosely in rib and re-join the side seam.

Diagram 176

To add extra length, unpick the seams to allow the work to lie flat. Pull out a thread right across the work immediately above the ribbing. Pick up the ribbed stitches (see diagram 176) and work the extra length, then graft the stitches together as shown below.

Grafting: Place the two sets of stitches to be joined parallel on two needles wrong side inside. Thread a tapestry needle with the same wool and join together thus: take tapestry needle knitwise through first stitch and drop stitch off needle, take tapestry needle purlwise through next stitch and leave this on knitting-needle. Take tapestry needle purlwise through first stitch on second knitting-needle and drop this stitch off needle, then take tapestry needle through next stitch on back needle knitwise and leave this on the knitting-needle. Continue in this way to the end, drawing stitches up to match the knitting.

To shorten a garment, unpick the seams to allow the work to lie flat. Pull out a thread right across the work, immediately above the section to be shortened. Unravel the amount required, then pick up the stitches and graft together as explained above.

If you cannot manage to graft the stitches off the needles, lay them side by side and graft as shown in diagram below.

Diagram 177: Flat grafting.

Blocking: This makes all the difference to the finished result. Each section must be pinned out to the measurements and pressed on the wrong side with a warm iron over a damp cloth. If a steam iron is being used, set it to a low temperature. Leave sections pinned until they are completely dry. Do not press ribbed sections.

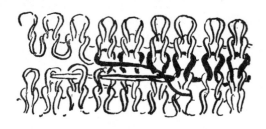

Diagram 177

Assembling: Use a tapestry needle and wool from the garment for sewing. If the wool is textured, use matching embroidery wool. Back-stitch (see diagram 3) edges together from the wrong side when joining sides, shoulders and sleeves. Ribbed sections should be edge-stitched. When setting in sleeves, pin the centre top to shoulder seam. Sew together from the armhole edge so that the back-stitching can be worked along the one row.

Storing Knitteds: Do not put garments on hangers but fold them and lay them flat if possible

Washing Knitteds: Do not use hot water and only use a little washing powder in the water. Squeeze the fabric gently to remove any stains. Rinse the garment thoroughly several times to remove any lather (this can cause shrinkage if left in the fabric). Roll the garment in a dry towel to remove excess moisture, then dry flat, away from direct heat (this would cause discolouration and possible shrinkage) or direct sun (this can fade wool and drain bleach from synthetics).

Abbreviations: These have to be used in most pattern writing in order to simplify the instructions. Sometimes special abbreviations are used in connection with cables and fancy patterns, but these are always explained in the pattern or abbreviations section. Care should be taken in referring to the abbreviations when unfamiliar patterns are being followed.

General Abbreviations: K. – knit; p. – purl; st., sts. – stitch, stitches; ins. – inches; inc. – increase (by working into front and back of same stitch); dec. – decrease (by working two stitches together); beg. – beginning; rep. – repeat; patt. – pattern; t.b.l. – through back of loop; m.1 – make one stitch (by winding wool round needle); st. st. – stocking-stitch (one row knit, one row purl alternately); g. st. – garter-stitch; (every row knit); m. st. – moss-stitch (k.1, p.1 alternately ending with an odd stitch); sl. – slip; p.s.s.o. – pass slip-stitch over; tog. – together.

Diagram 178: Casting On. Make a slip-knot as shown, pull the continuous wool up through the loop on to the knitting-needle. This forms the first stitch. Transfer the needle to the

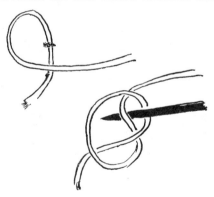

Diagram 178

left hand. Insert right-hand needle through this stitch, draw another loop through and place it on the left-hand needle.

Diagram 179. Add more stitches by inserting needle-point between the last two stitches and drawing out a loop for next

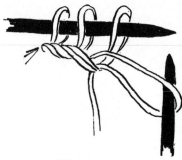

Diagram 179

stitch. Continue in this way until the required number of stitches are cast on. This method gives a double edge to the work which stands up to hard wear.

Diagram 180: Knit. Insert needle over front loop on left-hand needle through the stitch to the back of work. Wind wool over needle and draw loop through the stitch on to right-hand needle, at the same time dropping the stitch off the left-hand needle.

Diagram 181: Knit Through Back Loop. Take needle to the back of left-hand needle and insert it through the back of the stitch. Wind wool over needle and draw loop through the stitch on to right-hand needle, at the same time dropping the stitch off the left-hand needle – this method twists the stitch to the left.

Diagram 180

Diagram 181

Diagram 182: Garter-Stitch. This consists of knitting every stitch (see diagram 180) on every row, forming ridges on both sides of the work. This is the simplest form of knitting and most suitable for teaching beginners.

Diagram 183: Purl. Insert needle from back to front through the loop on left-hand needle. Wind wool over needle and draw loop back through the stitch on to the right-hand needle, at the same time dropping the stitch off the left-hand needle.

Diagram 184: Purl Through Back Loop. Take needle to the back of the left-hand needle and insert the needle through the

Diagram 182   Diagram 183   Diagram 184

back of the stitch from left to right (you may find it easier to draw the loop away from the left-hand needle with the point of the right-hand needle before inserting the needle through the stitch). Wind wool over needle and draw loop back through the stitch on to the right-hand needle, at the same time dropping the stitch off the left-hand needle.

Diagram 185: Pass-Slip Stitch Over. This method of decreasing has the same effect as 'Knit through the back loop' in appearance, but is often used in lacy patterns. Slip the relevant stitch from the left-hand needle to the right-hand needle (without working through it in any way). Work the next stitch as instructed in pattern, then use the point of the left-hand needle to lift the slipped stitch over the worked stitch and off the needle.

Diagram 186: Stocking-Stitch. This consists of one row knit (see diagram 180) and one row purl (see diagram 183) alternately throughout. It presents a smooth surface on the right side and rows of purl ridges on the wrong side.

Diagram 187: Single Rib. This is fairly elastic and used for

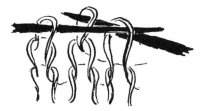

Diagram 185   Diagram 186

welts, cuffs and neckbands, etc. It consists of one stitch knit
(see diagram 180) and one stitch purl (see diagram 183)
throughout each row. It forms the same ridge pattern on each
side of work. The second row must be worked to correspond.

Diagram 188: Moss-Stitch. This consists of alternating knit
(see diagram 180) and purl (see diagram 183) stitches as shown.

Diagram 187   Diagram 188

KNITTED BATHMAT

Diagram 189. This simple pattern is quick to knit in easy
garter-stitch, with thick cotton. It is ideal for an absolute beginner to tackle. The cotton is very cheap to buy.

Materials: Twilleys Lyscot: 1 4-ounce hank each of white

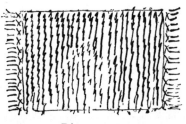

Diagram 189

and contrast; No. 2 knitting-needles; 1 yard of white cotton
towelling fringe (optional).

Measurements: 18 by 25 inches (excluding fringe).

Tension: 5 stitches to 2 inches and 4 rows to 1 inch.

Abbreviations: See page 159.

See general directions for knitting on page 155 before attempting the pattern.

To Make: With contrast cotton cast on 45 stitches. K. 4 rows. Join on white cotton. Do not break off the contrast, but carry in up the side of work, looping the working thread around it at the beginning of alternate rows. X With white, k. 4 rows. With contrast, k. 4 rows. Rep. from X 11 times. Cast off.

Diagram 190: Casting Off. Work 2 stitches. With point of left-hand needle lift the first stitch on the right-hand needle over the last one. Work 1 more stitch and continue lifting stitches off needle in the same way until only one stitch remains on the right-hand needle. Draw thread through this loop and fasten off. When accounting for the number of stitches cast off in patterns, do not include the stitch left on the needle and this should be counted in with the continuation stitches.

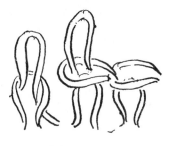

Diagram 190

Finishing Bathmat: Pin out to measurement and press the wrong side with a warm iron over a damp cloth. Darn in ends. Enclose each short end in the towelling fringe heading and neaten sides of fringe by turning in raw edge and oversewing (see diagram 12).

Alternatively remaining cotton may be cut into 8-inch lengths and hooked through each end for fringe (see diagram 167 for fringing).

KNITTED CLASSICS (see photographs between pages 86 and 87).

Instructions are given for all the popular classic styles for men, women and children – ranging in size to fit from 22-inch to 42-inch chest or bust measurement.

Each garment has fully fashioned raglan shaping and is easy to knit in stocking-stitch and rib.

See general directions for knitting on page 155 before attempting the patterns.

Note. Throughout instructions are given for the smallest size, with alterations for larger sizes in brackets. You will be able to pick out the instructions you need very quickly if you underline all the relevant figures in pencil.

Materials: Sirdar Double Knitting Wool for each garment in the undermentioned amounts. Two each Nos. 7 and 9 knitting needles.

Girl's Cardigan: 8 (9 : 10 : 11) ounces; 5 buttons.

Boy's Jumper: 8 (9 : 10 : 11) ounces.

Woman's Cardigan: 14 (15 : 16 : 17) ounces; 9 buttons.

Man's Sweater: 18 (19 : 20 : 20) ounces.

Measurements:

Girl's Cardigan: to fit up to a 22 (24 : 26 : 28)-in. chest; length, $14\frac{1}{2}$ ($15\frac{1}{2}$: $16\frac{1}{2}$: $17\frac{1}{2}$) ins.; sleeve seam, $10\frac{1}{2}$ ($12\frac{1}{2}$: $14\frac{1}{2}$: $16\frac{1}{2}$) ins.

Boy's Jumper: To fit up to a 22 (24 : 26 : 28)-in. chest; length, 16 (17 : 18 : 19) ins.; sleeve seam, 11 (13 : 15 : 17) ins.

Woman's Cardigan: to fit up to a 30 (32 : 34 : 36)-in. bust; length, 21 (21 : 22 : 22) ins.; sleeve seam, 17 (17 : 18 : 18) ins.

Man's Sweater: to fit up to a 36 (38 : 40 : 42)-in chest; length, 25 (25 : 26 : 26) ins.; sleeve seam, 19 (19 : 20 : 20) ins.

Tension: 11 sts. to 2 inches on No. 7 needles.

Abbreviations: Please see page 159.

GIRL'S CARDIGAN

The Back: With No. 9 needles cast on 64 (70 : 76 : 82) sts. X work 22 (24 : 24 : 24) rows in k. 1, p. 1 rib. Change to No. 7 needles and continue in st. st. until work measures $8\frac{1}{2}$ (9 : $9\frac{1}{2}$: 10) ins. from beg., ending p. X *Raglan Shaping.* Cast off 3 (3 : 3 : 3) sts. at beg. of next 2 rows. *Next Row.* K. 3, sl. 1, k. 1, p.s.s.o., k. to last 5 sts., k. 2 tog., k. 3. *Next Row.* P. Rep. last 2 rows until 18 (20 : 22 : 24) sts. remain. Cast off.

Left Front: With No. 9 needles cast on 30 (33 : 36 : 39) sts.
and work as given for back from X to X.
Raglan and Front Shaping. Next Row. Cast off 3 (3 : 3 : 3)
sts., k. to end. *Next Row.* P. XX. *Next Row.* K. 3, sl. 1, k. 1.
p.s.s.o., k. to end. *Next Row.* P. Rep. last 2 rows once. *Next row.*
K. 3, sl. 1, k. 1, p.s.s.o., k. to last 2 sts., k. 2 tog. *Next row.* P.
Rep. from XX until 7 (6 : 5 : 4) sts. remain. Continue to shape
raglan armhole only until 3 sts. remain. *Next row.* P. *Next row.*
K. 2 tog., k. 1. *Next row.* P. *Next row.* K. 2 tog. Fasten off.
Right Front: As left front up to raglan shaping, ending k.
Raglan and Front Shaping. Next row. Cast off 3 (3 : 3 : 3)
sts., p. to end XX. *Next row.* K. to last 5 sts., k. 2 tog., k. 3.
Next row. P. Rep. last 2 rows once. *Next row.* K. 2 tog., k. to
last 5 sts., k. 2 tog., k. 3. *Next row.* P. Rep. from XX until 7
(6 : 5 : 4) sts. remain. Continue to shape raglan armhole only
until 3 sts. remain. *Next row.* P. *Next row.* K. 2 tog., k. 1. *Next
row.* P. *Next row.* K. 2 tog. Fasten off.
Sleeves (both alike): With No. 9 needles cast on 42 (44 : 46 :
48) sts. and work 20 (20 : 22 : 22) rows in k. 1, p. 1 rib. Change
to No. 7 needles and continue in st. st., inc. 1 st. each end of
every 8th row until there are 54 (58 : 62 : 66) sts. Continue
straight until sleeve measures $10\frac{1}{2}$ ($12\frac{1}{2}$: $14\frac{1}{2}$: $16\frac{1}{2}$) ins., ending p. Shape top as for Back raglan until 8 (8 : 8 : 8) sts. remain,
ending p. Cast off.
Front Band: With No. 9 needles cast on 8 sts. Work 2 rows
k. 1, p. 1 rib. *Next row.* Rib 3, cast off 2 sts., rib to end. *Next
row.* Rib 3, cast on 2 sts., rib to end. Continue in rib, working 4
more buttonholes $2\frac{1}{4}$ ($2\frac{1}{4}$: $2\frac{3}{8}$: $2\frac{3}{8}$) ins. apart. Continue until
band is long enough to fit front edges, sleeve tops and back neck.
Cast off ribwise.
Making Up: Press work on wrong side with a warm iron
over a damp cloth, omitting ribbing. Join raglan shapings then
join side and sleeve seams. Sew on front band, placing buttonholes to right front for a girl and to left front for a boy. Press
seams. Sew on buttons to correspond with buttonholes.

BOY'S JUMPER

The Back: With No. 9 needles cast on 64 (70 : 76 : 82) sts. and work 12 (12 : 14 : 14) rows in k. 1, p. 1 rib. Change to No. 7 needles and continue in st. st. until work measures 10 (11 : 12 : 13) ins. from beg., ending p.

Raglan Shaping: Cast off 3 (3 : 3 : 3) sts, at beg. of next 2 rows. *Next row.* K. 3, sl. 1, k. 1, p.s.s.o., k. to last 5 sts., k. 2 tog., k. 3. *Next row.* K. 3, p. to last 3 sts., k. 3. Rep. last 2 rows until 20 (22 : 24 : 26) sts. remain. Leave sts. on a st. holder.

The Front: Work as Back until 36 (38 : 40 : 42) sts. remain in raglan shaping, ending with a wrong side row. *Next row.* K. 3, sl. 1, k. 1, p.s.s.o., k. 11 (11 : 11 : 11), cast off 4 (6 : 8 : 10) sts., k. to last 5 sts., k. 2 tog., k. 3. Continue on last set of sts. only. *Next row.* K. 3, p. to end. *Next row.* K. 2 tog., k. to last 5 sts., k. 2 tog., k. 3. Rep. last 2 rows until 5 (5 : 5 : 5) sts. remain, ending with a wrong side row. *Next row.* K. 3 tog., k. 2. *Next row.* K. *Next row.* K. 3 tog. Fasten off. Join wool to inner edge of remaining sts. *Next row.* P. to last 3 sts., k. 3. *Next row.* K. 3, sl. 1, k. 1, p.s.s.o., k. to last 2 sts., k. 2 tog. Rep. last 2 rows until 5 (5 : 5 : 5) sts. remain, ending with a wrong side row. *Next row.* K. 2, k. 3 tog. *Next row.* K. *Next row.* K. 3 tog. Fasten off.

Sleeves: With No. 9 needles cast on 34 (36 : 38 : 40) sts. and work 18 (18 : 20 : 20) rows in k. 1, p. 1 rib. Change to No. 7 needles and continue in st. st., inc. 1 st, each end of every 6th row until there are 54 (58 : 62 : 66) sts. Continue straight until sleeve measures 11 (13 : 15 : 17) ins., ending p. Shape top as for back raglan until 10 (10 : 10 : 10) sts. remain. Leave sts. on a st. holder.

Neckband: Join raglan shapings excepting left back. With No. 9 needles and with right side of work facing, k. sts. from left sleeve top, pick up and k. 18 (18 : 18 : 18) sts. down left side of neck, 4 (6 : 8 : 10) sts. from centre neck, and 18 (18 : 18 : 18) sts. up right side of neck, k. sts. from right sleeve top and from back neck. 80 (84 : 88 : 92) sts. Work 12 (12 :

14 : 14) rows in k. 1, p. 1 rib on these sts. Cast off loosely in rib.

Making Up: Press work on wrong side with a warm iron over a damp cloth, omitting ribbing. Join side and sleeve seams. Join neckband and left back seam, fold in half to inside and slip-stitch over pick-up row.

WOMAN'S CARDIGAN

The Back: With No. 9 needles cast on 90 (96 : 102 : 108) sts. X Work 22 (22 : 24 : 24) rows in k. 1, p. 1 rib. Change to No. 7 needles and continue in st. st. until work measures 11 (11 : 11½ : 11½) ins. from beg., ending p. X.

Raglan Shaping: Cast off 3 (3 : 3 : 3) sts. at beg. of next 2 rows. *Next row.* K. 3, sl. 1, k. 1, p.s.s.o., k. to last 5 sts., k. 2 tog., k. 3. *Next row.* P. Rep. last 2 rows until 22 (24 : 26 : 28) sts. remain. Leave sts. on a st. holder.

Left Front: With No. 9 needles cast on 42 (45 : 48 : 51) sts. and work as given for back from X to X.

Raglan Shaping: Next row. Cast off 3 (3 : 3 : 3) sts., k. to end. *Next row.* P. *Next row.* K. 3, sl. 1, k. 1, p.s.s.o., k. to end. Rep. last 2 rows until 12 (13 : 14 : 15) sts. remain.

Neck Shaping: Cast off 4 (5 : 6 : 7) sts., p. to end. *Next row.* K. 3, sl. 1, k. 1, p.s.s.o., k. to end. *Next row.* P. 2 tog., p. to end. Rep. last 2 rows once. *Next row.* K. 2, k. 2 tog. *Next row.* P. 2 tog., p. 1. *Next row.* K. 2 tog. Fasten off.

Right Front: As left front up to raglan shaping, ending k. *Next row.* Cast off 3 (3 : 3 : 3) sts., p. to end. *Next row.* K. to last 5 sts., k. 2 tog., k. 3. *Next row.* P. Rep. last 2 rows until 12 (13 : 14 : 15) sts. remain.

Neck Shaping: Next row. Cast off 4 (5 : 6 : 7) sts., k. to last 5 sts., k. 2 tog., k. 3. *Next row.* P. to last 2 sts., p. 2 tog. Rep. last 2 rows once. *Next row.* K. 2 tog., k. 2. *Next row.* P. 1, p. 2 tog. *Next row.* K. 2 tog. Fasten off.

Sleeves: With No. 9 needles cast on 50 (52 : 54 : 56) sts. and work 20 (20 : 22 : 22) rows in k. 1, p. 1 rib. Change to No. 7 needles and continue in st. st., inc. 1 st. each end of every 6th

row until there are 78 (82 : 86 : 90) sts. Continue straight until
sleeve measures 17 (17 : 18 : 18) ins., ending p. Shape top as
for back raglan until 10 (10 : 10 : 10) sts. remain. Leave sts.
on a spare needle.

Neckband: Join raglan shapings. With No. 9 needles and
with right side of work facing, pick up and k. 14 (15 : 16 : 17)
sts. from right neck edge, k. sts. from right sleeve top, back
neck and left sleeve top, then pick up and k. 14 (15 : 16 : 17)
sts. down left neck edge. 70 (74 : 78 : 82) sts. Work 8 rows in
k. 1, p. 1 rib. Cast off ribwise.

Buttonhole Band: With No. 9 needles cast on 8 sts. Work 4
rows in k. 1, p. 1 rib. *Next row.* Rib 3, cast off 2 sts., rib 3. *Next
row.* Rib 3, cast on 2 sts., rib 3. X Work $2\frac{1}{4}$ ($2\frac{1}{2}$: $2\frac{3}{8}$: $2\frac{3}{8}$) ins.
then make another buttonhole (measure from cast-on edge of
previous buttonhole). Rep. from X 7 times. Work 4 more rows
rib then cast off ribwise.

Button Band: With No. 9 needles cast on 8 sts. and work 20
(20 : 21 : 21) ins. in k. 1, p. 1 rib. Cast off ribwise.

Making Up: Press work on wrong side with a warm iron
over a damp cloth, omitting ribbing. Join side and sleeve seams.
Sew buttonhole band to right front edge and button band to
left front edge. Press seams. Sew on buttons to correspond
with buttonholes.

MAN'S SWEATER

The Back: With No. 9 needles cast on 106 (112 : 118 : 124)
sts. and work 20 (20 : 22 : 22) rows in k. 1, p. 1 rib. Change to
No. 7 needles and continue in st. st. until work measures $14\frac{1}{2}$
($14\frac{1}{2}$: 15 : 15) ins., ending p.

Raglan Shaping: Cast off 4 (4 : 4 : 4) sts. at beg. of next 2
rows. *Next row.* K. 3, sl. 1, k. 1, p.s.s.o., k. to last 5 sts., k. 2
tog., k. 3. *Next row.* P. Rep. last 2 rows until 26 (28 : 30 : 32)
sts. remain. Leave sts. on a st. holder.

Front: Work as back until raglan shaping.

Raglan and Neck Shaping: Next row. Cast off 4 (4 : 4 : 4)
sts., k. 47 (50 : 53 : 56) k. 2 tog., turn and leave remaining sts.
on a st. holder. X *Next row.* P. *Next row.* K. 3, sl. 1, k. 1,

p.s.s.o., k. to end. Rep. last 2 rows once. *Next row.* P. *Next row.* K. 3, sl. 1, k. 1, p.s.s.o., k. to last 2 sts., k. 2 tog. Rep. from X until 8 (7 : 6 : 5) sts. remain. XX Continue to shape raglan armhole only until 3 sts. remain. *Next row.* P. *Next row.* K. 2 tog., k. 1. *Next row.* P. *Next row.* K. 2 tog. Fasten off. Join wool to inner edge of remaining sts. *Next row.* K. 2 tog., k. to end. *Next row.* Cast off 4 (4 : 4 : 4) sts., p. to end. X *Next row.* K. to last 5 sts., k. 2 tog., k. 3. *Next row.* P. Rep. last 2 rows once. *Next row.* K. 2 tog., k. to last 5 sts., k. 2 tog., k. 3. *Next row.* P. Rep. from X until 8 (7 : 6 : 5) sts. remain. Complete as from XX on other side.

Sleeves : With No. 9 needles cast on 54 (56 : 58 : 60) sts. and work 22 (22 : 24 : 24) rows in k. 1, p. 1 rib. Change to No. 7 needles and continue in st. st., inc. 1 st. each end of every 6th row until there are 88 (92 : 96 : 100) sts. Continue straight until sleeve measures 19 (19 : 20 : 20) ins., ending p. Shape top as for back raglan until 8 (8 : 8 : 8) sts. remain. Leave sts. on a st. holder.

Neckband : Join raglan shapings, excepting left back. With No. 9 needles and with right side of work facing, k. sts. from left sleeve top, pick up and k. 52 (54 : 56 : 58) sts. down left neck edge, 1 st. from centre front and 52 (54 : 56 : 58) sts. up right neck edge. K. sts. from right sleeve top and back neck. 147 (153 : 159 : 165) sts.

1st row. (P. 1, k. 1) to end. *2nd row.* Rib 58 (60 : 62 : 64), k. 2 tog., t. b. l., k. 1, k. 2 tog., rib to end. Continue in rib, working 2 sts. tog. each side of centre front neck on every alternate row until 10 rows of rib have been worked altogether. Cast off loosely ribwise.

Making Up : Press work on wrong side with a warm iron over a damp cloth, omitting ribbing. Join side and sleeve seams. Join neckband and left back seam. Press seam.

CHAPTER 18

Crochet

IT is very useful to know how to crochet because it gives a professional finish to knitted garments (for borders) and lifts plain linens into the luxury class, with the addition of a lace edging.

In addition to the fine lace crochet, bulky wools can be used to make fashionable garments. Once you understand how this work is done, you will be able to choose patterns from current crochet leaflets or follow magazine instructions. Cobweb-fine lace patterns are issued by the manufacturers of the fine threads, and these are available from needlework departments.

Detailed instructions and working diagrams are given here for all the basic stitches. Practise each stitch, using a large hook and a thick thread so that you will be able to see quite clearly what you are working.

Materials: Always use the materials specified in the pattern. This is very important as the characteristics of the various threads and wools are considered in the original design. What is suitable for cotton is not always right for wool.

Cotton is available in a thickness to suit every purpose and can be used with confidence for household articles as it improves with washing. Steel crochet-hooks, in fine sizes, are generally used for cotton.

Crepe wool is most effective for crochet work – the high twist lessens the possibility of pilling which ruins the texture. For wools there are 'Aero' hooks, these are larger than the steel ones.

Make sure you have the right hook for the work in hand.

Tension: This must be correct as stated in the pattern, otherwise the work will not turn out the right size. Work a small piece of the pattern, using the right hook and thread. Place this flat and measure the stitches with a ruler and use pins to mark the stitches for counting. If there are too few stitches, try a smaller hook; and if there are too many stitches, try a larger hook. Do not attempt the pattern until you have the right tension.

Joining Thread: Do not make knots in the work. When you see that the thread is running out, lay the new thread along the top of work and work a few stitches over this, then release the finishing thread and work over this with the new thread in the same way.

Working: The secret of success with crochet lies in the holding of the hook and the working thread. There is always a tendency to pull the thread too tight when learning to crochet.

Hold the hook between the thumb and forefinger of the right hand, and hold the working thread between the third and fourth fingers of the left hand and bring it over the second finger. The thumb and forefinger of the left hand are used to hold the crochet work in position for the hook. Keep the working thread under control by extending the left-hand second finger, thus allowing sufficient space for the hook to be put over and under the extended thread for every stitch.

Initial Loop: This is made in the same way as for knitting and is shown in diagram 178.

Diagram 191: Chain. This forms the foundation of crochet

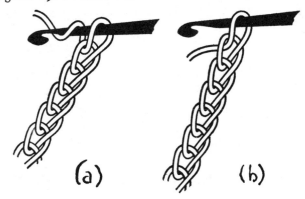

(a)   (b)

Diagram 191

work, and beginners should practise chain-stitch until all the stitches are of a uniform size and the hook slips easily through the stitches. Start with a slip-stitch loop and hold hook and thread as described above. (*a*) Pass the hook under the thread held in left hand and catch the thread with the hook. (*b*) Draw thread through loop on hook. Repeat this movement until chain is required length.

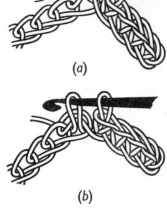

(*a*)

(*b*)

Diagram 192

Diagram 192: Slip-Stitch. Insert hook into stitch to the left of hook, catch thread with hook and draw through stitch and loop on hook.

Diagram 193: Double Crochet. (*a*) Insert hook into stitch to the left of hook, catch thread with hook. (*b*) Draw thread through stitch (two loops now on hook). (*c*) Thread over hook and draw through two loops on hook (only one loop remains on hook).

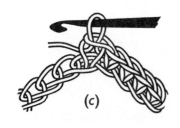

(*c*)

Diagram 193

Diagram 194: Treble. (*a*) Pass hook under the thread of left hand. (*b*) Insert hook into stitch to the left of hook, thread over hook and pull through stitch (three loops on hook), thread over hook. (*c*) Pull through two loops on hook, thread over hook, (*d*) Pull through remaining two loops (one loop remains on hook).

Abbreviations: Ch. – chain; s.s. – slip-stitch; d.c. – double crochet; tr. – treble; p. – picot; inc. – increase (this is usually done by working twice into the one stitch); dec. – decrease (this is done by missing one of the stitches in the previous row, or by working two stitches together); tog. – together; rep. – repeat; patt. – pattern; sp. – space; bl. – block; gr. – group.

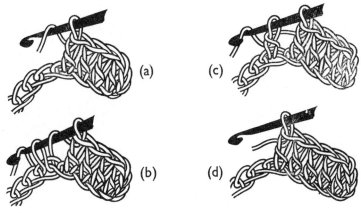

(a)   (c)

(b)   (d)

Diagram 194

CHAIN-STITCH CUSHION

Diagram 195. This is a perfect sample for a beginner to tackle. It can be quickly made and consists entirely of the basic chain-stitch.

Materials: 1 pound of rug wool and a No. 5 Aero crochet-hook; matching thread.

Measurements: 15-inch diameter circle.

To Make: Crochet a continuous length of chain (see diagram 191) for about 3 yards. Do not break off wool. Start to coil the chain (with the top of stitch facing inwards) into a flat circle and sew the rows of chain together with matching thread.

Diagram 195

Keep the work on a flat surface to coil the chain. Continue in this way until circle is 15 inches in diameter, crocheting more chain if necessary. Break off rug wool and darn in ends.

Make another circle in exactly the same way.

Making Up : Press work on wrong side with a warm iron over a damp cloth. Make a cushion-pad as described on page 127. With crochet-hook slip-stitch (see diagram 192) the two circles together all round edge, enclosing the pad.

Trimming : S.s. to join rug wool (4 ch., miss 1 st., s.s. in next st.) all round. Fasten off neatly.

PICOT EDGING

Diagram 196. This dainty edging is particularly suitable for lawn handkerchiefs (if you wish to make one, use a 9½-inch square of lawn).

Diagram 196

Materials : Coats Mercer-Crochet No. 40 and a steel crochet-hook No. 4½; work over rolled edge or through drawn threads.

Abbreviations : See page 173.

Edging : Work one row of d.c. all round edges, working 3 d.c. in each corner. *Next round.* (3 ch., s.s. to 2nd ch. from hook, 1 ch., miss 2 d.c., s.s. in each of next 2 d.c.) to end. Fasten off. Darn in end. Press edging with a hot iron over a damp cloth.

FILET CROCHET

Diagram 197 : (a) *Edging* (b) *Insertion* (c) *Motif.* This simple pattern, consisting of chain and treble, can be used in several

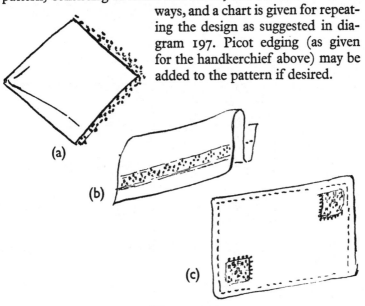

ways, and a chart is given for repeating the design as suggested in diagram 197. Picot edging (as given for the handkerchief above) may be added to the pattern if desired.

(a)

(b)

(c)

Diagram 197

Diagram 198 : Filet Crochet Chart.

Materials : Coats' Mercer-Crochet No. 20; Milward's steel crochet hook No. 3.

Measurement: ½-inch wide (but may be worked with thicker cotton and larger hook if desired).

Abbreviations : Please see page 173.

Edging : Make 15 ch. *1st row.* 1 tr. in 8th ch., (2 ch., miss 2 sts., 1 tr. in next st. – referred to as 1 sp.) twice, 5 ch., turn. *2nd row.* Miss 2 ch., 1 tr. in each of next 4 sts. – referred to as 1 bl.– 1 sp., 3 ch., turn. *3rd row.* 1 tr. in each of next 3 sts., 1 sp., 1 bl., 5 ch., turn. *4th row.* Miss 2 sts., 1 bl., 1 sp., 5 ch., turn. *5th row.* Miss 2 sts., 1 tr. in next st., 2 sp., 5 ch., turn. Rep. last 4 rows for patt. throughout length required.

Insertion: Start with 23 ch. and follow two sections of chart.

Motif: Start with 32 ch. and follow chart to make square pattern.

Dampen crochet and pin out to dry, or press with a hot iron over a damp cloth.

Diagram 198

SHELL EDGING

Diagram 199. This is a pretty edging for a plain garment. It can be crocheted on a foundation of chain and applied, or worked directly into the fabric of the garment.

Diagram 199

The Pattern: Make a length of chain divisible by 6. X Miss 2 ch. (1 tr., 1 ch.) 3 times in next ch., 1 tr. in same ch., miss 2 ch., s.s. in next ch.; rep. from X throughout.

If this is being worked directly on to the garment, leave the length of the tr. st. between the group and s.s.

MOTIF CROCHET CUSHION
(see photograph beween pages 86 and 87).

This dainty motif could be built up to any size and would make a lovely blouse. Make a paper pattern of the shape and arrange motifs to fill the area. The motifs could be seamed through to shape the shoulders, etc.

Each flower has a darned centre, which is done with a needle when the crochet work is complete.

Materials: 6 ounces Sirdar Fontein Crepe; No. 1 Aero crochet-hook.

Measurements: Cushion, 15 inches square; each motif, 1½ inches.

Abbreviations: Please see page 173.

First Motif: Wind wool six times round left index finger, then remove loops and s.s. around the strands. *1st round.* 24 d.c. in ring, s.s. to first d.c. XX *2nd round.* 8 ch., X (1 tr. in each of next 3 d.c., 3 ch., 1 tr. in each of next 3 d.c., 5 ch.) 3 times, 1 tr. in each of next 3 d.c., 3 ch., 1 tr. in each of next 2 d.c., s.s. to 3rd ch. Fasten off, leaving 10 inches for centre darning.

Centre: From wrong side of crochet, darn across the centre 5 times in each direction (see diagram 139).

Second Motif: Work as given for first motif up to XX. *2nd round.* 5 ch., 1 d.c. in corner loop of first motif, 2 ch., 1 tr. in each of next 3 d.c. on second motif., 1 ch., 1 d.c. in next 3 ch. loop on first motif, 1 ch., 1 tr. in each of next 3 d.c. on second motif, 2 ch., 1 d.c. in next corner loop on first motif, 2 ch. Complete from X as first motif. Darn centre.

Make 16 more motifs and join each one as second was joined to first motif. Now make eight more rows of 18 motifs, joining successive motifs along two sides.

Making Up: Press work on wrong side with a warm iron over a damp cloth. Fold in half across the width, join corners and centres of each motif all round, enclosing a cushion pad before finally closing side. For making cushion pad see page 127.

CROCHET FLOWER TRIM

Diagram 200. Pretty trimming for little girl's party clothes or hair grips. They could be made in raffia for summer and wool for winter.

Abbreviations: Please see page 173.

Flower: Make 8 ch. and join into ring with s.s. *Next round.* X 1 d.c. in next ch. (2 ch. 1 tr.) 3 times in next ch.; 2 ch.; rep. from X three times. Fasten off.

Sew a small shank pearl button to centre.

Diagram 200

PATCHWORK CROCHET

Diagram 201. This pattern is ideal for a practical cot cover or for a glamorous fringed stole. You can use oddments of wool or work the motifs in two dramatic shades as shown.

Use Double Knitting Wool and a No. 8 crochet-hook for a 3-inch square.

Abbreviations: Please see page 173.

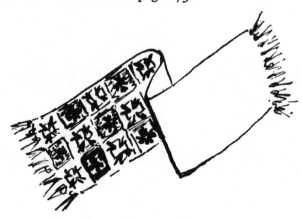

Diagram 201

Motif: Make 8 ch. and s.s. to join into ring. *1st round.* 3 ch., 2 tr. in ring (1 ch., 3 tr.), 3 times in ring, 1 ch., s.s. to 3rd ch. S.s. back into 1 ch. sp. *2nd round.* (3 ch., 2 tr., 1 ch., 3 tr.) in same sp., X 1 ch. (3 tr., 1 ch., 3 tr.), in next 1 ch. sp.; rep. from X twice, 1 ch., s.s. to 3rd ch. S.s. back to 1 ch. sp. *3rd round.* 3 ch., 2 tr. in same sp., X 1 ch. (3 tr., 1 ch., 3 tr.), in corner sp., 1 ch., 3 tr. in next sp.; rep. from X three times, omitting 1 ch. 3 tr. at end, 1 ch., s.s. to 3rd ch. Fasten off.

Alternate Motif: Use contrast wool for 1st and 3rd rounds, main colour for 2nd round only.

Press work on wrong side with a warm iron over a damp cloth. Join motifs together on wrong side, stitching through every crochet-stitch on each motif.

If required for a stole, see diagram 167 for fringing.

TRICOT STITCH

Diagram 202. This is worked with a special hook which is longer than ordinary crochet-hooks. Also, a blanket needle is used if making a large article, such as a blanket.

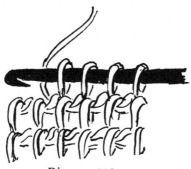

Diagram 202

The texture is cellular so it is soft and light for baby blankets and the stitch grows quickly.

The stitch is worked in two movements – forward, when all the stitches are picked up on to the hook, and return, when each stitch is worked off the hook.

Materials (for a double-bed blanket): $3\frac{1}{2}$ pounds winter weight blanket wool (or $2\frac{1}{2}$ pounds of summer weight wool); a blanket needle (adjustable to three lengths); 9 yards of satin blanket binding.

Measurements : 65 by 87 inches.

Tension : 7 sts. to 3 inches.

Abbreviations : Please see page 173.

Make 150 ch. (the length of chain decides the width of blanket). *1st row. Forward movement.* Miss 1 ch. (insert hook in back of next ch., draw wool through and leave loop on hook) to end. *Return movement.* Wool over hook, draw through first loop (wool over hook, draw through two loops) to end. *Next row. Forward.* Insert hook in back of 2nd upright st., draw loop through and leave loop on hook (insert hook in back of next upright st., draw loop through and leave loop on hook) to end. Work return movement as given in 1st row. Rep. last row until work measures 87 inches. Fasten off.

Making Up : Bind blanket as given for Baby Blanket on page 6.

Note. When working tricot stitch keep the loops loose throughout, drawing each one up to about $\frac{1}{2}$ inch in the forward movement and making the stitches in the return movement as loose.

Part 6

JIFFY GIFTS

CHAPTER 19

Jiffy Gifts

SMALL gifts are needed all the year round – for birthdays and bazaars. If you can make these yourself you will save money and also you will find that it is an enjoyable pastime.

Several of the ideas included here are simple enough for children to implement, and most of the gifts can be made from scraps of material or wool. All of them are quick and easy to make.

DOLL'S DRESS (see photograph between pages 118 and 119).

This is made from four straight pieces, all in easy garter-stitch. The inexpensive doll measures 12 inches, but the dress could be adapted to fit any size.

Materials: Double knitting wool, 1 ounce main colour and $\frac{1}{4}$ ounce contrast; No. 9 knitting-needles; 3 small buttons.

Tension: 6 sts. and 10 rows to 1 inch.

Abbreviations: Please see page 159.

See general directions for knitting on page 155.

Bodice Front: With main colour cast on 20 sts. and work 30 rows in g. st. (every row k.). Cast off.

Bodice Back (2 pieces alike): With main colour cast on 20 sts. and work 16 rows in g. st. Cast off.

Skirt: With main colour cast on 8 sts. and k. 2 rows. Join contrast. Do not break off main colour, but carry it along the side of work to use when required. With contrast, k. 4 rows. Continue in this way, working 2 rows main colour and 4 rows contrast, until there are 31 stripes altogether – one for every ridge in the bodice. Cast off.

Making Up : Press work with a warm iron over a damp cloth. Join one back piece on to each side of front bodice, leaving 1 inch open at top edge (for armholes). Join on skirt section, slip-stitching through each ridge on lower edge of bodice and through the top of one pleat in the skirt. *Embroidery :* With contrast work two lazy-daisy flowers (see diagram 34) with french knot centres (see diagram 31) and straight-stitch leaves and stem (see diagram 42) down centre front of dress.

Join shoulder seams, sloping seam ½ inch, to armhole edge, for ½ inch. Join skirt seam. Work three buttonhole loops along right back edge (see diagram 203). Sew buttons to left back edge to correspond with loops.

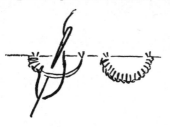

Diagram 203

Diagram 203: Buttonhole loops. Work two or three loops through edge of fabric, large enough to go over button, then work buttonhole-stitch (see diagram 20) over loops.

PLACE MAT AND NAPKIN

Diagram 204. Embroidered braid trims this practical set which is quick and easy to sew.

Materials : A piece of linen 11 by 14 inches for mat and an

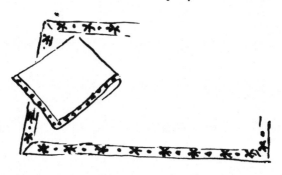

Diagram 204

11-inch square for napkin; 3 yards of 1-inch-wide embroidered braid; matching sewing-thread.

Measurements : Mat, 10 by 13 inches; napkin, 10 inches square.

To Make : Turn in ½ inch all round to right side of linen. Pin edge of braid to fold, mitring the corners (see diagram 7). Machine-stitch each edge of braid or work running-stitch (see diagram 6) if sewing by hand. Press work on wrong side with a hot iron.

BRIDGE MOTIFS

Diagram 205. Work these in cross-stitch (see diagram 25) on gingham with ⅛-inch squares. Work one cross-stitch in each square on the fabric.

These motifs may be worked on a bridge cloth or napkins, bound with matching bias (see diagram 5). Use six strands of thread in needle for the embroidery.

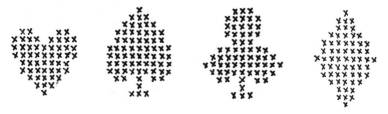

Diagram 205

PRAM SHEET AND PILLOW CASE

Diagram 206. Baby linen is always an acceptable gift and it is expensive to buy already trimmed.

You can buy a plain set and trim it with *Broderie Anglaise.* Use 1-inch wide frilling for

Diagram 206

pillow case ($1\frac{1}{2}$ times the measurement for fullness in gathering) and 3-inch wide insertion for sheet. The insertion should be sewn to top of sheet, 1 inch from edge.

This set will be much admired and the sheet will help to keep the pram cover from getting soiled from baby handling.

FABRIC FRAME

This is an inexpensive way of framing a print and it adds much to its value as a gift.

Cut stiff card to required size, then remove centre, leaving the width desired. Use this card frame to cut out material, leaving $\frac{1}{2}$-inch turnings on outer and inner edge.

Clip fabric diagonally up to $\frac{1}{2}$ inch in each corner inside frame.

Fold fabric over card to wrong side and sew from side to side all round, taking needle through edge of inside and outside seam allowance alternately. Make sure that the stitching is pulled evenly and that the fabric is lying straight on the right side.

Paste this frame on wrong side and mount over print. Back with stiff card cut to $\frac{1}{4}$ inch of shape. Insert picture rings through card back before pasting this over framed print.

NURSERY MOTIF

Diagram 207: Donkey Motif Chart.

This would make a fascinating panel for a small child. Work two donkeys, facing each other, or a string of donkeys on brightly coloured even-weave linen. See diagram 25 for cross-stitch, diagram 34 for lazy-daisy stitch and diagram 33 for Holbein stitch.

Work one cross stitch over two threads in each direction and use 4 strands of embroidery thread in needle. If you use fabric with 16 threads to 1 inch the motif will measure 3 by 4 inches.

Diagram 207

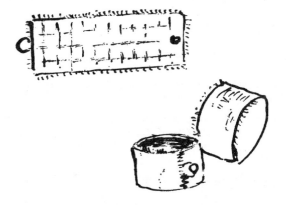

Diagram 208

NAPKIN HOLDERS

Diagram 208. Quick-to-make napkin holders, in gay colours, would save confusion at home. They would also be useful for identifying napkins used by weekend guests.

Materials : For each napkin holder, a strip of Binca canvas, 2 by 6 inches, a small button and some matching sewing-thread.

To Make : Draw away one square of threads all round. Sew a button one end and make a buttonhole loop the other (see diagram 203).

DARNED EMBROIDERY

Diagram 209. Binca canvas is ideal for teaching little girls to sew. Cut out a small mat, say 6 inches square, and give the child some gay threads to darn in and out of the tiny holes.

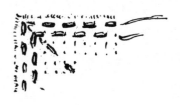

Pearl cotton would be better than stranded embroidery thread for this purpose as it is easier to handle.

No hem is needed and the edges may be fringed as desired. The finished mats could be used as drip mats for glasses, or china.

Diagram 209

LAVENDER BAG

These can be made from scraps of ribbon, about 2 by 6 inches wide, and edged with dainty lace.

Fold ribbon in half, across width, right side outside, and oversew sides together (see diagram 12 for oversewing). Fill bag with lavender, turn in remaining edges and oversew. Gather narrow lace ($1\frac{1}{2}$ times the measurement all round lavender bag) by drawing up the thread in the straight edge of lace to fit edge. Join short ends neatly then sew gathered lace to edge.

PIN CUSHION

Diagram 210. This is a popular bazaar-make. Use brilliant felt for the cushion cover and fill it with clippings of felt, foam rubber or carpet felt.

To Make : Using household objects mark a 3-inch and 4-inch circle on different colour felt. Cut out circles with a pinking shears (which will serrate the edges).

Cut out a flower motif from cotton fabric, if available, and *appliqué* this (see diagram 45) to centre of smaller circle. Alternatively embroider a flower in stem-stitch (see diagram 41).

Diagram 210

Place felt circles together and stab-stitch these together (see diagram 10) $\frac{1}{4}$ inch from edge of inner circle, enclosing filling before finally closing seam.

EVENING BAG

Diagram 211. Diamanté trimmed satin bag.

It is very easy to make an envelope-type bag for special occasions. A small piece of left-over dress material could be used.

Materials : A piece of satin, lining and stiff canvas, each $10\frac{1}{2}$ by $12\frac{1}{2}$ inches: two pieces in the same materials 4 by 5 inches (for side gussets); matching sewing-thread and $\frac{1}{4}$ yard of diamanté trimming.

Diagram 211

To Make : Place satin and lining together, right sides inside. Cover with canvas interlining and join together $\frac{1}{2}$ inch from edge on one short and two long sides. Trim seam and turn out to right side. Turn in remaining raw edges and oversew opening. See diagram 12 for oversewing.

Join gusset sections together in the same way. Fold each gusset piece in half lengthways and oversew one short end together. Place the open end of gusset to the overcast edge of the bag piece and oversew the gusset side edge to the side edge of bag, pushing the joined end of gusset inside the fold of bag.

Fold top flap over sewn section and trim lower edge of flap with diamanté.

PAMPERED PUSSYCAT (see photograph between pages 118 and 119).

This enchanting creature is made from evenly-wound balls of wool and sits in a raffia basket.

Materials : 2 ounces of white double knitting wool; a scrap of pink felt and 5 inches of $\frac{1}{2}$-inch-wide pink ribbon; a few pearl beads for necklace and ear-rings; 1 needleful of brown embroidery thread (for features); natural raffia and matching sewing-thread (for basket).

Measurement : 5 inches tall.

To Make : Wind wool tightly and neatly into a 2-inch ball for head and a 3-inch ball for body. Fasten off ends securely, oversewing the final twists of wool to prevent them slipping afterwards. Sew head to body. *Ears :* Cut pink felt $1\frac{1}{2}$ by 1 inch and round off one long edge for tip of ear then sew ears in position along straight edge. *Nose and Mouth :* Cut $\frac{1}{4}$-inch triangles and sew apex-to-apex to face. Embroider eyelids $\frac{1}{2}$ inch wide in stem-stitch (see diagram 41). Work eyelashes, eyebrows and whiskers in straight-stitch. *Tail :* Cut pink felt 1 by 3 inches. Roll this strip and hem the outer edge (see diagram 8 for hemming). Sew tail to body and tie bow around tip as shown. Sew one pearl bead to each ear and tie beads around neck.

MINIATURE MOUSE (see photograph between pages 118 and 119.)

Make this from pink fur fabric and white felt. The tiny skirt is optional. The actual size pattern is given here.

Materials: Pink fur fabric 6 inches square; a 4-inch square of white felt; 12 inches of 1-inch wide *Broderie Anglaise* edging (for skirt); two small beads and flower sequins (for eyes) and a few strands of necklace nylon for whiskers. Matching sewing-thread and kapok for stuffing; a pipe cleaner.

Measurement: $3\frac{1}{2}$ inches tall.

Diagram 212. Actual-size pattern.

Cutting Out. Trace off actual-size pattern given in diagram 212. Cut two pieces of pink fur fabric for body (*a*) reversing the pattern for the second section, so that the fur fabric strokes from front to back of pattern on both pieces. Cut (*b*) in fur fabric for head gusset, with fur fabric stroking from point X. From white felt cut front body (*c*), placing straight edge to fold, cut two pieces (*d*) for ears and two pieces (*e*) for tail.

Making Up: Pin gusset between head pieces, matching pile direction, from X. Sew gusset in position from wrong side, making seam $\frac{1}{4}$ inch from edge in back-stitch (see diagram 3). Sew front neck seam and also back and underbody seam in the same way. Clip curves and turn out to right side.

Stuff body through front opening. Pin front body over opening, $\frac{1}{4}$ inch over edge of fur fabric all round. Hem felt in place (see diagram 8 for hemming). Sew ears to back of head along straight edge. Sew bead over sequin flower to head for eyes each side of head. Sew nylon to face for whiskers – secure this with loop-stitch round base of each strand. Oversew the tail pieces together (see diagram 12) enclosing the folded pipe-cleaner. Sew tail to back of body. *Skirt.* Join short ends of *Broderie Anglaise.* Gather top edge and draw up to fit body then fasten off.

BOBBLE BIRDS (see photographs between pages 118 and 119)

These lovable birds are made from pom-pons and children would enjoy making them in gay colours.

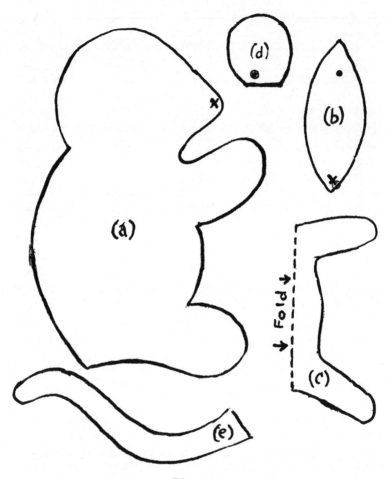

Diagram 212

Materials: 1 ounce each of pale and dark blue double knitting wool and a small quantity of lemon wool (sufficient for
both birds); scraps of orange and brown felt; two card circles
in each of the following sizes: 2 inches and 3 inches (for large
bird), $1\frac{3}{4}$ and $2\frac{3}{4}$ inches (for small bird); a 15-inch piece of $1\frac{1}{2}$-
inch-wide blue lace for large bird's tail.

Measurements: Large bird 5 inches tall and small bird 4 inches.

To Make: Large Bird. Cut ⅓ away from centre of card circles. *Body:* Use large card circles. See page 109 for making pom-pons. Wind pale blue first until centre circle is half filled then complete with dark blue. *Head:* Wind ⅓ of circle only in pale blue then complete with lemon wool. Sew head to body. Cut a 1-inch square of orange felt and fold diagonally and sew to head for beak. Sew ¼-inch circles of brown felt for eyes and mark eyelashes in brown thread. Gather lace and sew to back of body for tail. *Small Bird.* Cut ⅓ away from centre of card circles. *Body:* Use large card circles. Wind pale blue first until centre circle is half filled then fill in a further quarter with dark blue and finally fill with pale blue. *Head:* As large bird. Make up as large bird, but sew a pale blue tassel (see page 108) for tail and a ½-inch square for beak.

Index